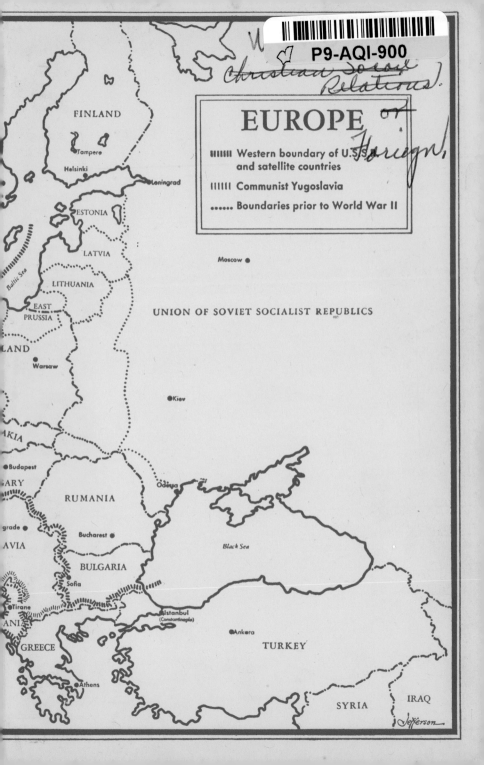

Christian Europe

by STEWART WINFIELD HERMAN

author of IT'S YOUR SOULS WE WANT &
THE REBIRTH OF THE GERMAN CHURCH

FRIENDSHIP PRESS • NEW YORK

To MY WIFE

whose love speaks volumes

Contents

Author's Preface

EUROPE refuses to be left out of account. Today we talk as though the whole world were divided into two halves, but that is only a part truth. All of Europe—not merely the Western part!—continues to play a fateful and major role between the East and the West. Divided Germany illustrates the point exactly. But non-Communist Asia and Africa must also be reckoned with, if we are ever to reach a clear comprehension of the interplay of world powers. Witness the crucial significance of the Middle East! There are at least four main factors involved in present-day tensions leading either to peace or to war: the United States, the USSR, Europe, and Asia.

Of these four factors, Europe is far more important than we think. How much do we really know about it? In the thinking of the average North American, the Old World functions alternately as a delightful playground for tourists or as a grim battlefield for soldiers. For those who are neither tourists nor soldiers, the bewildering variety of ancient and modern Europe constitutes an arsenal of confusing evidence to support any point of view or way of life that you care to adopt. In short, it appears to be all things to all men. But this is not necessarily the Europe that the European sees. Above all, it is not the way the Christian European looks at his country or his continent. To him Europe is no more bewildering than America is to the American.

The object of this book is not to consider the whole state of the church in the world today but, as soberly as possible, to assess the role of religion in Europe today. My primary purpose has been to throw some additional light on a few of the broader and deeper issues confronting the church, without attempting to prove either that the Christian faith is doomed in Europe or that it is on the verge of a smashing victory.

North Americans, to whom this volume is primarily directed, have been casually crossing the ocean for many generations, but their fund of information about Christian Europe is probably less comprehensive than their knowledge of Christian Asia or Christian Africa. It is equally true, of course, that Europeans know relatively little about Christian America. Missionary interests have led the Christians in both Europe and America to become more familiar with their brethren on the other side of the world than on the other side of the Atlantic. This is a great pity, because a larger measure of Christian solidarity in recent decades might have helped to guide the course of political and economic events into more peaceful waters. It must not be forgotten that Europe and North America together constitute the two most influential Christian continents in the world today.

One aspect of America's emergence from relative isolation as regards European affairs is the growing desire of the man and woman in the pew to know more about the workings and the problems of the European church today. For several postwar years church members of all denominations have gladly sent food, clothing, and money for the rehabilitation of Europe's church life. Gradually they have come to ask themselves a major question: What is Christian Europe really like?

It was very difficult to decide, in view of the requisite brevity, whether to describe the churches of Europe on a country-by-country basis (which tends to become monotonous) or to describe major Christian issues without reference to geographical demarcations (which can become confusing and vague). Finally, it was decided to combine the two ideas by trying to fit five major subjects in five European areas (Chapters Four to Eight inclusive).

A division of this sort is bound to be artificial, because it is obvious that a treatment of the state-church question, for example, should not be confined solely to Scandinavia, nor the impression be given that Roman Catholicism is something that can be localized in Italy and Spain. Yet, on the whole, the present outline seemed to offer the best opportunity to survey Christian Europe, and I trust that readers will make due allowances for the fact that certain extremely interesting countries, such as the Netherlands, Austria, and Czechoslovakia, receive but little explicit attention. A much larger volume would have been required to do justice to every country.

Some readers, especially if they happen to be Europeans or ardent friends of Europe, may come to the conclusion that I have been unduly "American" in my effort to describe the status of the Christian churches in Europe today and the issues that they face. Other readers, who may harbor strong convictions—as I do—about such questions as complete separation of church and state, the importance of consecrated personal stewardship, or the vital significance of each congregation in the attainment of a truly Christian society, may undoubtedly feel that I have paid too much attention to the vast, reverberating cathedral churches of Europe, for example, and too little attention to the chapel denominations or the aggressive postwar gospel movements.

To both groups of readers, I can only say that I have endeavored to present a reasonably clear analysis of Christian Europe *as it actually is*. Despite the fact that I have known Europe intimately for seventeen years, this is not exactly easy for an American to do, but I have had the assistance of a wide circle of friends from many countries who have frequently corrected my vision. Sitting down to discuss this manuscript with them proved to be invaluable, and I wish herewith to express my gratitude to at least a dozen men and women—especially in the World Council of Churches—who have read various chapters and given me their comments. Although they would not wish to be made responsible for it, they have certainly helped to write this inadequate guide to the unfamiliar parts of betraveled Europe.

There are undoubtedly many things that we American Christians have in common with our European brethren, and there are likewise many things in which we are strangers to each other. So far as these latter things are concerned, it would be of especial benefit to scrutinize them carefully with a view to getting better acquainted. The church in Europe, which has received so much from us, has much to give. Perhaps we have more to offer than we thought. I am speaking of an exchange of spiritual gifts. Christianity on both continents has developed some characteristic features, in contact with dissimilar environments. Europe today is inclined to borrow a few ideas from America. On the other hand, Europe has acquired a very costly fund of Christian experience— in addition to its theological erudition—during the course of these last years. It behooves both of us to pool all the knowledge we have, because there are large areas of life on both sides of the Atlantic where the impact of Christian faith is seldom, if ever, felt.

STEWART WINFIELD HERMAN

Geneva, Switzerland

1

The European Phoenix

No DOUBT the most familiar aspect of postwar Europe is the panorama of destruction that, when unrolled before church audiences, resulted in an unprecedented flood of funds for relief and reconstruction. It is impossible to say how much has been given. In 1951, five full years after the end of the war, the annual contributions to Europe's Protestant and Orthodox churches, according to the World Council of Churches, totaled $9 million in goods and cash. Most of this was still coming from the United States, but by no means all. Canada, Australia, Brazil, and Argentina stand out among the most prominent overseas contributors to the rehabilitation of Europe and the revival of its churches.

The German Protestant Hilfswerk, which has been a major recipient of relief supplies in Europe, issued a report late in 1951 acknowledging the receipt of 69,300 tons of relief goods from 22 different countries since 1945, easily worth $50 million. The United States led the list with 45,100 tons, but Sweden came second with 13,700 tons and Switzerland third with 4,000 tons. When you consider that Sweden has a population of only 7 million people and Switzerland about 4 million, the gifts of these smaller countries— by comparison—take on heroic proportions. In addition, all three nations have dispatched countless quantities of individual food parcels and money gifts.

WHAT KIND OF RECOVERY?

Gradually a new panorama of recovery has been superimposed upon the panorama of destruction, showing a revived Europe rapidly arising from the old ashes and ready to resume its full political and economic share in world affairs. Travelers returning from summer tours describe the hotels, the shops, the abundance of luxury goods available for dollars and conclude that as far as foreign aid is concerned the postwar emergency is over. To a certain extent this is true, but tourists often do not realize that much of the physical recovery they see is simply a screen behind which the rest of Europe's rubble can be hidden.

Shortly after the war it was estimated that many decades would be required merely to clear away the mountain of debris. Today, surprisingly enough, the heavily bombed city of Kiel is 90 per cent cleared of its wartime wreckage. Pforzheim in South Germany, which was 70 per cent destroyed, has shaken off 600,000 cubic meters of rubbish and put up 4,500 new apartments. The Protestant Home Building Society alone has completed over 8,000 dwelling units, mostly apartments, all over Western Germany. Endless data of this sort is available. Can it be assumed, however, that Europe's spiritual recovery is keeping pace with this economic recovery and doing nicely? Or does the naive attitude of the summer travelers laden with souvenirs imply that the economic recovery of Europe is America's business but that its spiritual recovery is not?

The answer to the first question is definitely negative: Europe's spiritual recovery is not keeping pace with its economic recovery. The answer to the second question must necessarily be conditioned by one's point of view. Is it any of our business? I dare say that no traveler who has taken the time to look behind the brave new façades of European reconstruction has turned away feeling that what he saw there was none of his business—not if his hope is for peace. His purse then becomes less important than his prayers, for only a fraction of mankind's problems can be solved by cash.

The churches of Europe are busily engaged in repairing the physical damage they suffered. But today the troubled Christians of Europe are not solely or even primarily concerned with the burden of debris or the costs of its removal. To be sure, Holland had 400 churches destroyed or damaged; Poland lost 100, and 200 were heavily damaged; Hungary lost 40, and 600 were heavily damaged; France lost 72 entirely, and 140 were heavily damaged; Germany lost over 600, with 823 partially destroyed and 1,832 damaged!

These figures are by no means complete, because the time has never been taken to tabulate all the statistics on the war's destruction. They refer only to houses of worship, mostly Protestant, at that. They do not begin to tell the whole story of parsonages wrecked; orphanages, hospitals, and other institutions bombed out or burned up; equipment ruined or looted; and lives lost or crippled. In the North Rhine Province of Germany only 10 per cent of all church property remained untouched by war damage. Church leaders are not unduly depressed by the fact that much of what has been destroyed cannot possibly be restored. The future usefulness of the numerous and lonely old burnt-out churches deep in the City of London, for example, has had to be rigorously considered before reconstruction begins. Only a few will be rebuilt for normal parish purposes in sparsely populated neighborhoods; others will be restored as guild chapels and some not at all.

THE CHURCHES SLOWLY RISE AGAIN

It is gratifying to note that the physical property of the church has been fairly well patched up to meet present needs in Europe, thanks partly to foreign help but largely to the perseverance of local members. In postwar Germany a modest chapel frequently stands beside the ruins of an ancient and often empty structure, or—as in the Eastern Zone—some part of a huge skeleton has been sealed off to serve indefinitely as a chapel-in-the-church. In less than five years Hilfswerk alone set up 126 barracks chapels and "rubble" churches all over Germany. This same organization, by appealing to the Protestant congregations, had collected more than 150 million reichsmarks for self-help projects before the end of 1947! By the beginning of 1951 about 50 per cent of the 1,500 damaged church properties in Berlin-Brandenburg, including parsonages and parish houses, had been returned to regular use!

It almost seems as though the further east one goes the more complete the repairs have been. The rebuilding of churches in England and Norway had hardly started when the report came from Hungary that every damaged church had been repaired or rebuilt.

Even more remarkable than the speed of reconstruction is the self-sacrifice with which the churches in many parts of the impoverished continent have struggled to re-establish themselves. In March, 1951, the Church Rebuilding Fund in Greece made an appeal for $4 million to rebuild 800 churches ravaged in its postwar war, and within a few months collected half of the total. The fact that one million dollars represents about 15 billion drachmae provides some conception of the extent of Greek inflation.

The worst destruction in Scandinavia had been wrought in the arctic areas of Norway and Finland by the withdrawal of the German Army across Lapland to the Atlantic coast. Every church building in that sparsely-settled area was destroyed. In 1951 the Finns completed—with U. S. Lutheran help—the repair of the last seven structures and thus wiped out their losses, having raised twice as much money (60 million finmarks) in their church-wide Common Responsibility Offering as they had anticipated.

Building priorities made church reconstruction in Norway more difficult, but foreign gifts right after the war enabled "chapel boats" to serve the isolated towns and villages that were destined to wait ten years for their new churches. Four of them were finally dedicated in the summer of 1951.

Meanwhile, both Norway and Denmark had long since rejoined Sweden in returning to the ranks of the "giving" churches. Vast quantities of relief goods and large sums of money have been raised to speed up the rehabilitation of Central Europe. Part of these gifts have come from the state treasury but a very large part from freewill offerings sponsored by the churches. By 1951 the Protestant churches of little Holland were contributing $30,000 worth of goods and cash to refugees in Germany, in addition to sponsoring 8,000 refugee children in summer camps and giving permanent homes to 103 "hard core" DP's. Special tribute should be paid both to the government and to the Reformed churches of Switzerland, which have carried an amazing part of the relief and reconstruction work in postwar Europe.

THE REFUGEES—CHURCHLESS AND HOMELESS

The problem of devastation and reconstruction was bad enough, but the problem of refugees was, of course, infinitely worse. Nearly 15 million uprooted people were scattered over Western Europe, mostly in Germany, where every second family is still living without decent accommodations, owing to the fact that more than one-third of the housing was destroyed. One-third of West Germany's more than one million unemployed persons are refugees and several millions must be counted destitute and in need of public assistance. It was inevitable that a new migration agency had to be set up in 1952, after the closure of the International Refugee Organization. Its purpose is to relieve the economy of Europe by assisting the emigration of tens of thousands of people from areas of Europe that contain ten to twenty times as many inhabitants per square mile as there are in North America. By reliable estimate, one authority has come to the astounding conclusion that since 1945 in Europe alone at least 27 million people have lost their former homes.

Yet even the refugees have, to a surprising degree, helped themselves as far as they could. Take, for example, the expellees from Czechoslovakia who happened to land in an abandoned munitions dump in the Bavarian Forest! Since 1946, when the first families crowded into a few crude barracks and cooked over campfires, the community has grown into an industrious parish of 2,400 souls supported by 120 commercial enterprises. They employ 900 men workers and keep 500 women busily occupied with home handicrafts with an annual turnover of about $4 million. This takes leadership, but such leadership is relatively rare.

In these new communities, the church frequently stands at the center of life—in contrast to the famous model "churchless" town that was built in Hitler's time to house the workers of the Nazi Volkswagen factory. Today there are churches in such towns, too!

THE FINANCIAL PLIGHT OF PASTORS AND PEOPLE

When due allowance has been made for Europe's remarkable economic recovery, it must be said that most Europeans are still living from hand to mouth in financial straits that the average American family, accustomed as it is to automobiles and television sets, would find difficult to imagine. This is especially true of Great Britain, where fewer than 100 people are reported to be earning more than $15,000 per year and the average Anglican clergyman receives a basic salary of $1,500. It is also true of France and Austria where the cost of living rose 30 per cent in 1951, now rivaling the cost in the United States, but where pastors are paid only $60 per month, which is much less than $1,000 per year, not counting housing and very meager family allowances. Pastors' salaries are quoted for two reasons: first, because they reflect the general plight of all white-collar workers; secondly, as an index to the financial situation of the church. It is a rare pastor anywhere in Europe who earns the equivalent of $2,500 and it is doubtful whether many Protestant bishops are much better off.

Eighty per cent of the German people have a monthly income of about 300 DM, or less than $70. When you add the fact that in many countries all savings, as well as a tremendous percentage of accumulated wealth in the form of property and household goods, have been wiped out, the penury becomes almost tangible. In Austria and Germany especially provision had to be made for the hundreds of ethnic German pastors who were evacuated or fled with their people. In some instances, salaries of all regular pastors were reduced 10 to 15 per cent to cover the cost of a modest monthly allowance to the men from the East, their widows, and their orphaned children. The small Austrian church, despite a generous grant from abroad, met two-thirds of the cost of these extra salaries itself.

STEWARDSHIP VERSUS TAXES

Under the above-mentioned circumstances it becomes almost embarrassing to follow up the flood of Christian funds from America with pep talks about stewardship. Yet many Europeans freely deplore the fact that the vast majority of even their most active church members—except in some free churches—have no acute sense of responsibility for the financial support of the church and its work. Tithing is regarded as wholly fantastic. The payment of church taxes is usually accepted even by disinterested persons as a legitimate charge on regular income for maintaining religion.

In Bavaria about two-thirds of the total Lutheran budget was met from church taxes in 1950, less than 10 per cent from collections, and the remainder from various other sources, chiefly obligations acknowledged by the state. The average per capita church tax was 6.70 DM (less than $1.50) but it must be remembered that this is spread out over the whole nominally Protestant population, including children. In addition, an average of 4.50 DM (about $1.00) per year is placed voluntarily on various offering plates by those who attend church. Collections for many major activities do not normally appear in the church books. The total income for the same church in 1949 was 27,600,000 DM, or nearly $7 million from its 2,400,000 baptized members.

Needless to say, these taxes are very low, but they are not always paid cheerfully. The situation in Austria illuminates the predicament of the Protestant churches throughout Europe. In 1938 the Austrian church balanced its budget fairly well. Today church taxes, which constitute almost the entire income, cover only one-quarter of the needs laid down in an adequate church budget. This meager tax represents about one-hundredth (a tithe of a tithe!) of the income, and must be collected by the church itself. Many families—pressed by economic distress—try to evade it just as they try to evade the income tax itself. The vast majority of Austrians probably earn less than $600 per year. Out of 1,000 church tax accounts in one parish, two widows offered to give more, 500 persons paid without murmuring, 200 to 300 haggled and bargained before paying, and the remainder refused. The writer of an article in an Austrian church paper asks whether it is really a sacrifice to give as much as 10 schillings (30 cents) per month, if you spend 100 schillings on cigarettes. The line of argument sounds familiar.

All over Europe, it may be said, an increasing interest is being shown in general voluntary support of church work for a wide variety of reasons. Bishop Otto Dibelius of Berlin appealed for free-will offerings for the training of catechists, not only for the specific purpose of supplementing the church income that was totally unable to meet the need, but also to train church members against the day when the entire support of the church may fall upon their individual gifts.[1] Today the voluntary *opfergroschen,* which is used for religious instruction, represents less than 3 per cent of the amount received from church taxes. Giving takes practice.

One of the most interesting reactions to American Christian donations in the postwar period is the universal surprise that tremendous sums of money can be raised—and that all Christian activity can be paid for—by the voluntary offerings of active parish members. As Dean H. C. Asmussen of Kiel has said, "I am less inclined to see the wealth of our American brethren in their dollars than in the fact that they understand better than I do how man's redemptive action follows from God's redeeming love."

EUROPE RESUMES ITS FOREIGN MISSION ACTIVITY

At the same time, it is a common American failing to suppose that Europeans give nothing to the Christian cause except through taxes. This is an oversimplification, to say the least, and does not take into account the support of many Christian charities not formally attached to the church; nor, for example, the ardent support given to the great independent European societies for their extensive work in foreign missions throughout the world. Sweden alone supports 5 different fields that, in addition to 381 elementary schools and other educational projects, have 4 large hospitals and a number of smaller ones. All of the established churches have managed to do a great deal of mission work.

[1] Late in 1952 the East German Government took the first step to deprive the church of public help in collecting church dues.

Too frequently it has been assumed that nine-tenths of the foreign mission work, in Asia and Africa, for example, was being borne by North American and British societies. As a matter of fact, the churches of continental Europe have played a most important part in the extension of Christianity into many corners of the globe, especially India, Southeast Asia, and Africa. Some of the largest of the younger churches are the rich fruit of intense activity that was maintained not by church taxes or government subsidies but by the free-will offerings of interested members, just as in the United States. Funds were and are collected in a variety of ways, chiefly by organizing huge mission festivals that annually—on a high spiritual level—attract thousands of people who share the work to the point of self-sacrifice. During the war, when funds could no longer be transferred, the International Missionary Council stepped in to help. In the years between the outbreak of the war in 1939 and the end of 1951, almost $10 million was poured into the temporary support of orphaned missions, quite aside from the money raised for reconstruction inside Europe.

The support of the fields is being resumed, and there is an oversupply of missionary candidates ready to enter the service. Germany, in fact, has been able to send out approximately 100 missionaries since the end of the war and large new sums of money have been raised exclusively for the foreign mission work. Unfortunately, currency restrictions have hampered large transfers to the field, so that German, French, and Dutch societies continue to depend on outside help in maintaining their mission programs.

ALL HOPE IS CHRISTIAN

Once more Europe seems bent on demonstrating its physical indestructibility. When one reviews the bloody history of the little continent, it seems impossible to believe that this cradle of our modern civilization can withstand another major war. As a civilization, perhaps it won't. But suppose the rest of it does succumb to Soviet pressure and falls behind the Iron Curtain? Whether this seems likely or unlikely, one must never lose sight of the fact that Europe will cease to be Europe only when the last of its Christian substance is dissolved and disappears entirely. Communism may accomplish this, but many more generations would probably be needed to complete the process. For the brightest colors in the rich tapestry of old Europe are its Christian threads, and they will last the longest. Is the fate of Europe hanging by these threads? If Europe can no longer save the church, can the church save Europe?

Europe may not be indestructible, but Christianity is. The growing struggle of the European church against overwhelming odds is well worth the full support of her daughter churches around the globe. Christianity in Europe is not fighting some separate battle. In effect, it has faced and is still facing the same enemy that the church has always faced. That enemy is human sin. War's destruction and the lack of sufficient funds for reconstruction are lesser evils. Even American Christians are prone to believe that all of Europe's spiritual ills can be cured by money, and that by giving money we can cure ourselves. Sometimes European pastors and church leaders have given support to that misconception by the nature of their requests for help. Today it is becoming evident that gifts of another kind should be exchanged more freely: namely, the finer fruits of Christian faith and action.

In order to come nearer to this theme, all reference to the physical condition of the Christian church in postwar Europe has been compressed into this brief chapter. There is no shortage of data on the material problems that still plague the continent, but far more needs to be said about the subtler issues confronting Christian Europe. And more must be said of the victories already won.

2

Signs of New Spiritual Life

We are ripe for a religious revival, and I hope it will be crude!—European Manufacturer.

Our problem is, therefore, how to get in touch again with the masses of the "unfaithful faithful."—Professor Regin Prenter, Denmark.

THE greatest religious *discovery* of the twentieth century is that Europe, the cradle of Christian culture, is its own *major* mission field. Contrary to the sentences cited above, revival is not enough. Some Europeans, having accepted this missionary challenge as a cardinal reality, no longer regard its discovery as startling. Others, conscious that Europe has always been a fertile field for evangelization, resolutely refuse to take alarm at what appears to be nothing more than a slight increase in the number of backsliders. In order to place the proper emphasis in the first sentence, I have italicized the two most important words. Europe is rediscovering herself.

Two world wars and the half century in which they occurred have thrown a totally different light upon a continent that for centuries took its Christianity for granted. Today it is doubtful whether even the culture of Europe can be called Christian. Millions of Europeans are not merely outside the church but outside of Christendom itself; that is, they have been born and brought up in a non-Christian environment. Thus, they are beyond the reach of ordinary "revival" methods, for revival assumes that religious life is dormant and can be awakened. Although the churches, especially in the West, continue to enjoy the respect generally reserved for elderly spinsters, most of them are alien, if not dead, to the life of the people around them. In the Communist East they are publicly treated as superfluous, a tolerated nuisance.

DEAD-TIRED, BUT NOT DEAD

Painful as the discovery has been, the church in Europe is not yet ready to be consigned to the oblivion that the secular world seems so ready to thrust upon it. Like a gnarled and knotted tree that bears the scars of many a violent winter storm, the apparently indestructible church of Christ today compels the reluctant respect and admiration of many who regard the old veteran as dead wood. The sturdy trunk not only stands, but its gale-combed branches show new signs of life coursing from the roots of faith.

It is indeed exhilarating to observe almost everywhere in the old continent a fresh enthusiasm for evangelization and a determination to restore some Christian order to the world. For the first time in one hundred years, Christian Europeans show even more interest in their own spiritual condition than in that of Asians and Africans. Under the circumstances, that is a good sign, but let us not confuse these incipient buds with the ripe fruit, because by old-fashioned revival standards there is a deplorable absence of visible religious vitality in most European countries. With the exception of Finland and Hungary, it cannot be said that whole nations have felt the impact of an evangelistic movement in this generation, let alone in the five or six postwar years. Indeed, the goal of today's evangelists seems to be much more modest. What is important is that *radical experiments in Christian behavior are taking the place of eloquent preaching.*

Most of Europe's churches emerged from World War II in a state of exhaustion rather than elation. Pastors and people were physically and mentally weary. Thousands of Christian buildings—the precious heritage of untold generations—lay wrecked or ruined, and the communities that knew them had been uprooted not only in the course of forced evacuations but as a result of wartime industrial dislocations. The tedious task of rebuilding, brick by brick, the whole elaborate fabric of the Christian church was more than an impoverished and homeless generation could possibly face.

As wanderers in an unrecognizable world, Europe's millions needed tabernacles before they could dream of churches. When brought face to face with the ugly, cold, hungry reality of the postwar period, liberty itself sometimes seemed to be a luxury that they could ill afford to enjoy.

In only one case, as far as I know, did the whole Protestant church experience a nationwide revival, namely, in Russian-occupied Hungary. In the midst of a spiraling inflation, which finally shattered the old currency, devoted souls surrendered even their small stocks of precious gold to rebuild their houses of worship. As the only example of a national awakening in postwar Europe, this remarkable old-fashioned Hungarian revival deserves more than passing notice, because it may also prove to be the last of its kind in Europe, at least in our day.

ONE AUTHENTIC FLAME OF REVIVAL FIRE

Just after the war I traveled over a large part of liberated Europe without discovering any signs of a public revival—the natural fruit, as I thought, of the resistance movements in which Christian leaders played a prominent part. Then, in the fall of 1946, my visits brought me to shattered Budapest, where I found, quite unexpectedly, exactly what I had been looking for. Although the gov-

ernment was nominally in the hands of the Small-holders' Party
and the President of the republic was a former Reformed pastor,
there was no doubt that the real power was already firmly in the
grip of Rakosi, the Communist. The wealthy nobility had been dis-
possessed, the big estates had been cut up and divided among land-
less peasants, monuments to the Red Army were sprouting everywhere, and Russian soldiers were much in evidence. Yet the air itself seemed full of a new Christian confidence, especially in the
Protestant churches, and the pastors and bishops were en route
night and day attending revival services involving whole communities.

Two Reformation rallies in Budapest at the end of October took
the form of mass manifestations that were neither pro-Communist
nor anti-Communist. They witnessed a vibrant faith. High government officials of the interim regime were prominently present to
breathe the air of repentance, resolution, and renewal that per-
vaded the huge civic auditorium.

This revival movement really had its roots, I was told, in the
prewar period, not in wartime resistance. But it was intensified by
the war and by military defeat, to say nothing of the social shock
administered by Bolshevism in overturning the most feudal social
system in Europe. It aimed to convert not only isolated individuals
but whole parishes, and was a combination of personal evangelism
leading to conversion plus congregational reconstruction leading to
a new concept of the community.

Nowhere else in Europe, including Germany, was there so much
emphasis on the need for repentance. The Hungarians really
seemed to believe that they were being punished by God, not that
they should simply pay lip service to the idea. Consequently, the
various evangelistic impulses from Wesleyan England and Lutheran Finland that for years had been held at arm's length by

ecclesiastical conservatism swept into the church and took charge. Under the impact of defeat and a desire for total change, the same revival movement began to show certain social aspects. In this field, however, the Christian leaders were amateurs compared with the professional "reformers" trained in Marxist thought. The character of the whole awakening remained predominantly "spiritual."

This in itself was a remarkable exhibition of Christian renewal, as we shall soon see by comparison with the rest of Europe. The religious upsurge in Hungary, however, persisted so strongly that prominent visitors, and indeed some Hungarians themselves, were misled into thinking that contact with communism was the cause of it. The fact is that in pre-Communist Eastern Europe the core of Christian tradition was still comparatively sound, and, especially in the non-Orthodox churches, the effects of nineteenth century piety were plainly to be seen even in people who had lost interest in the local church. But as the Communist grip tightened, the evangelistic movement in Hungary inevitably declined.

REPLANTING THE CHURCH IN ERODED SOIL

Vienna is not very far from Budapest, but it lies on the other side of that invisible frontier that has always separated East from West in Europe. Here the attempts of the church to reach the world have already taken it out of the parish proper and into the alien neighborhood. In the "red" suburb of Semmering an evangelistic campaign was conducted by three teams, each consisting of two Lutheran pastors, who invited the workers into familiar surroundings—a refugee barracks, a public hall, a neighborhood restaurant— for informal discussions on life's personal problems. This is characteristic of modern Europe.

The further west you come the less you hear of evangelism beginning with a gospel call to personal repentance and the more you find it struggling to make contact with the surrounding community on any level that the indifferent public understands. It is rare that you can start with religious discussions. Theological systems of thought find no popular echo. Nor does ordinary evangelism have the power to reach the unchurched European. Sometimes it restores the man who has almost slipped beyond reach, but it rarely brings in those who have lost contact with Christendom.

The postwar mood requires motion. Tabernacles, not temples! A static church attracts no interest, let alone the maintenance of expensive ecclesiastical machinery that so easily crumbles under the impersonal fist of war. A few good films and plays have exercised far more evangelistic influence than the well planned revival campaigns, especially in Germany. Religious film commissions all over Europe are busily experimenting with this new medium for proclaiming a Christian message to a non-church public.

One of the most effective postwar plays in Germany, *The Sign of Jonah,* dwelt upon the inability of three "average" people to comprehend that they bore a share of responsibility for the development of events leading up to the war—the "what-could-I-do?" attitude. They first heaped the blame for their predicament on allied bombers, then on Hitler, then on the Treaty of Versailles, and, by gradual process of elimination, on God himself for permitting such disasters and misery. They think that God should taste this bitter suffering himself, yes, lose his own Son as they had lost their sons. Suddenly, as they argue it out, it dawns upon them that this has already happened!

Under the magnetic leadership of Bishop Hanns Lilje, who in August, 1952, was elected president of the Lutheran World Federation, a mobile attack is being made upon the province of Hanover, which comprises most of Northwest Germany. With German thoroughness a preparatory team moves into a typical town or city

and sets up a week's program that is designed to enlist the interest
and participation of every inhabitant, from the mayor to the
smallest child. People are approached along the line of their life
interest—the fireman in the firehouse, the worker in his factory,
the doctors and lawyers through their professional associations,
housewives, youths, and others. The aim of this Kirchliche Woche,
when all plans have been completed, is to make the entire community conscious of the fact that the church still stands at its center
and that it represents Christian values of incalculable worth to the
local and national community. Bishop Lilje joins his team when
the big Church Week begins and addresses himself daily to every
group, but the essence of his evening messages is contained in a
series of three simple but extremely effective talks on the Christian
faith as it is summarized in the Apostles' Creed.

One of the most impressive and spectacular attempts to put
religion in the forefront of the public consciousness is the gigantic
Kirchentag (Christian Congress), which the Protestants hold each
year in a different German city. The Roman Catholics have a somewhat similar festival. In 1950 the Protestants descended on Essen
in the Ruhr valley—200,000 strong—to prove that "it is possible in
the twentieth century to take Christianity seriously." In 1951 scores
of thousands of people came to Berlin, from both the East and the
West, for a tremendous assembly that devoted a full week to discussing four main issues of Christian life in huge "study groups"
containing at least 10,000 people each! On the final Sunday there
was a mammoth expression of Christian unity in the huge Olympic
Stadium. The Kirchentag is not intended to be a revival meeting,
but there can be no doubt that all those who have the experience
of attending it go home with a new sense of strength through
common fellowship.

The effectiveness of this tremendous mass meeting, which combines a genuine appeal to the individual with a powerful show of strength, must be seen to be believed. Its guiding spirit is Dr. Reinold von Thadden, a consecrated layman who in 1928 was made president of the German Christian Student Movement and later became European vice-president of the World's Student Christian Federation. During the last war he was commander of the district of Louvain, the famous Belgian university city, during the German occupation, but was so thoroughly Christian in his conduct that he was officially invited to return at the end of the war as the city's honored guest. Meanwhile he had lost his family estate to the Communists and had been taken prisoner in Russia for several months. When I first saw him in a Berlin hospital shortly after his release from this captivity, it seemed doubtful that he would ever recover from the effects of it. But today the mammoth and impressive Kirchentag—in 1952 it met at Stuttgart—is von Thadden's reply to those who think of Christianity as something that cringes fearfully in the corners of a darkened church.

WHO IS MY NEIGHBOR?

Europeans in general, and Christian Germans in particular, badly need a release from individual isolationism into a new sense of community fellowship. Down in conservative Bavaria some parishes have inaugurated Neighborhood Evenings. These foster Christian association on an informal basis by meeting in the more familiar surroundings of a local restaurant for a cup of coffee. In one city parish that averaged only 7 to 10 per cent attendance at the worship services, invitations were sent to a few score members in a certain street or district and as many as 20 to 45 per cent put in an appearance to meet one another as neighbors and talk with the pastor. As a result, fresh interest was aroused and the life of the whole parish was effectively reinforced. In the huge apartment houses of large German cities, fellowship such as this is to be warmly welcomed. Thousands of uprooted refugees have profited by it.

France, on the other hand, seems to be heading toward a radical repudiation of any and all attempts to refurbish old evangelistic techniques that are simply designed to entice people back into the same old church. Such efforts to revive the local congregation never seem to last longer than a halfhearted attempt to improve attendance on Sunday mornings by "brightening up" the service. Time-hallowed tricks for infusing fresh enthusiasm into other parish activities have also lost their magic.

In the final analysis, this type of revivalism is based on a premise that is no longer true: namely, that the church is still the natural center of the community and that the community is one big Christian family. Today the individual family in the community unquestionably continues to be the biological unit of society, but the factory, the club, the school, and other centers of activity have combined to split the home and have thus become the hubs around which family life revolves.

To serve the people who have become wholly attached to these modern social centers, the church, it is believed, must enter into the life offered by the factory, the mill, the labor union, or the other immediate interests of the community. Roman Catholic priests have sometimes taken secular occupations as miners, factory workers, or seamen in order to share the daily round with people to whom the church and cassock mean absolutely nothing. Some of them have even become sympathetically involved in Communist riots. Consecrated young Protestants are developing still further the missionary methods introduced by the McAll Mission tactics eighty years ago, but instead of hiring neutral halls in which to hold discussions first and then services, they do not even mention religion to people whose minds are closed.[1] Thus, part-time evangelism committees have given way to full-time Christian teams (*équipes*), which plunge into a churchless environment to render some urgent social service that may be quite unrelated to the usual activities of ordinary parishes.

France's main problem is to galvanize with living faith a vast population that cannot be said to have left the church but for more than a century has had nothing to do with it. Renewed efforts are today being made to reach them, as well as the tens of thousands of strangers who in the postwar years have drifted into France seeking refuge.

A special opportunity was given to young French Christians to accept this new responsibility when the population of Alsace was evacuated into central France during the war. The intention was to prevent the complete dissolution of disbanded parishes during their enforced exile. The first CIMADE teams, as they were called from the initials of their name, began to reorganize youth work and to assist the distraught pastors of the scattered flocks. Subsequently, the idea was successfully applied to towns devastated by the D-Day invasion and to more than a dozen camps housing the political refugees, Spanish republicans, interned Communists, and others. This led eventually to an international exchange of team members as a contribution to ecumenical understanding and international peace.

Much might be said, also, of several other French movements, the JEEP, La Main Tendue (The Outstretched Hand), the Protestant Family Association that is based on the idea that a team of families can often cooperate to do what single families cannot, and the Protestant Professional Association that attempts to regain the intellectual *élite*. But, as these latter two names suggest, we

[1] See Chapter 4.

are already touching again the groups that a tenuous thread still holds to the church, not those who have lost all contact.

Radical departures from the accepted techniques of evangelism have been explored also by British churches in an effort to break out of their religious ghetto into the workaday world. During the war Britain blazed some new trails, which the churches of postwar Europe, allowing for differences in their spiritual terrain, have sought to follow. When chaplains went back into the armed forces during the war, it was considered of equal importance to supply chaplains to the laboring forces in the big industrial centers on the home front. At one time more than 300 ordained pastors were assigned to the munitions plants and other factories to minister to the workers.

The Methodists, whose evangelistic zeal at the beginning of the nineteenth century undoubtedly was a major factor in preventing the complete secularization of Britain, inaugurated Commando Campaigns that "raided" the factories, the public houses (saloons), and amusement centers to try to reach the man beyond the short radius of the local church.

In two successive years, 1948 and 1949, London itself was the major objective of a Commando Campaign, followed by a city-wide Anglican Mission, but all of these efforts—valuable though they have been—serve only to confirm the conviction that what the non-Christian world needs is not a rousing revival but a new missionary conquest. Here again the best proposal seems to be to replant small groups of Christians—whether you call them teams or cells or priest-workers—in the center of society where they are left unencumbered by ecclesiastical machinery, to see whether some new form of church life will take root and flourish.

In Britain it was found that the industrial chaplains were frequently successful in winning the hearts of the workers, but rarely could the converted workers be brought into the fellowship of existing churches. This experience seems to be quite general in Western Europe. In Saxony in Eastern Germany 22 full-time men and women Christian workers are engaged in the mining areas. The conclusion to be drawn is that new programs for the training of Christian laymen must be instituted. The function of the new laymen would be not to hold the last line of defense against modern society, but to become the binding link between the churches and the world! Church and world, admittedly, must be moved closer together. If revivalism is no longer able to move the world, the church itself must move.

It seems to be the consensus in Europe, including the Vatican pronouncements, that the church must take the initiative in covering most of the intervening distance between it and its alien environment. No one is seriously advocating a more worldly church. On the other hand, any effort to achieve a more Christian world will certainly involve important changes in the parish patterns with which we are familiar—changes just as revolutionary, for example, as the radical but necessary difference between the first century fellowship and medieval monasticism, or between the Holy Roman Empire and the Reformation.

RE-ENLISTING THE LAYMEN IN HOLLAND AND FINLAND

The evangelization of de-christianized Europe in this era is not primarily a job for ordained preachers but for the working laymen, those silent servants of God's word whose daily lives speak louder than their lips. Even if all clergymen were entirely suitable for the task that lies ahead—despite the distinctive garments they wear, the facial expressions they frequently affect, and the vocabulary that their training has imposed—their total number is far too small to make a perceptible dent on the millions who must be reached.

Besides, there is a growing appreciation in Europe of the Biblical fact that the propagation of the Christian faith was never intended to be the exclusive prerogative of an ordained ministry. Laymen, of course, have always occupied positions of importance in the European churches—frequently as church presidents—but their function has usually been administrative rather than missionary. Today this, too, is changing.

The new use of laymen (and incidentally there is a strong tendency to abolish the word layman altogether) takes on two forms: keeping the trained Christian as a witness in his regular vocation; and giving him a special full-time function in the community.

Outstanding among the experiments to train young people for full-time Christian service is the Kerk en Wereld Institute of the Reformed Church in Holland. Here, during a two-year course, young men and women without university education are prepared to become parish assistants, but not so much for work among the members of the parish as among those who live within the parish but do not belong to it.

This evangelistic effort is strongly reinforced in a bi-weekly paper called *The Open Door*, which constitutes one of the best modern examples of systematic evangelization by mail, because the primary purpose of its distribution by laymen is to establish contact with those completely outside the church. Undoubtedly the Dutch churches provide an exception to the general rule that the spirit of resistance that flamed up during the Nazi occupation faded away without giving a firm new impetus to Christian revival. The Reformed Church is not suffering from any shortage of regular pastors, but it clearly saw, as a result of the ideological invasion, that Christian faith had actually been losing ground in the Netherlands.

Elsewhere in Europe similar training schools have been opened.

Owing to the lack of sufficient pastors in Alsace, the graduates of the recently-founded Martin Bucer Institute at Strasbourg ought to constitute a valuable addition to the church staff, but there is also the technical problem of fitting this new category of ministers into the state church system. Up in Finland two new institutes for the training of both full-time and part-time church workers—one in the Swedish language—have been established recently.

The basic idea of Luther College at Järvenpaa, near Helsinki, is to give young people a two-year course to prepare them for responsible leadership in the local congregation, but the school also serves as a Christian center for refresher courses, Sunday school teachers' seminars, conferences of pastors' wives and fiancées, high school study groups, and so on. In Finland, perhaps more than in any other European country, the strong impact of early nineteenth century revivals can still be felt. The memory of Paavo Ruotsalainen, the great peasant evangelist who united all the revivals and integrated them into the church life of the nation, was widely honored on the centenary of his death in January, 1952. From here a strong pietistic tributary swelled and helped to give direction to the evangelistic wave that, as we noted earlier, lately moved through Hungary.

Another movement of significance in Finland is known by the name Kansanraamattuseura, the pronunciation of which becomes somewhat easier when translated as People's Bible Society. Founded in 1945 under the leadership of Bishop Gulin, it presently employs 12 full-time evangelists and 40 other workers whose main job is to conduct evangelistic services in the congregations and reach the individual by personal counseling, confession, and absolution. In 1952 over 300 parishes were ready to make use of this postwar instrument to stir up again the religious life of communities all over the country. Two of the evangelists recently exchanged visits with

American Lutheran preachers, thus perpetuating Finland's tradition of carrying its efforts at Christian revival beyond the national border.

THE CREATION OF THE EVANGELICAL ACADEMIES

Training centers for laymen are not exactly new, but the idea has been seized upon and tremendously developed in these postwar years. One of the most notable is the Ecumenical Institute of the World Council of Churches at Bossey near Geneva. The forerunners of such institutes are to be found at Sigtuna in Sweden, and, in a slightly different sense, in the Iona Community on the historic island of that name off the west coast of Scotland. Both of these places have for years exercised a powerful and steady evangelistic influence, not unlike the first creative impact of medieval monasteries on the formation of Christian community patterns. These institutes also have a very fruitful contact with each other on an international basis, which quickly places the valuable results of one of them at the disposal of all.

The Evangelical academies that sprang up all over Germany after the war under the auspices of provincial churches adapted these plans for lay training to the regeneration of Christianity in a shattered and defeated country. According to the leader of the Bad Boll Academy, two things had to be corrected: the remoteness of the church from the world and its lack of roots in the laity. The strategic solution to the whole problem was to bring people together for a few days or, if possible, for a few weeks, to think in terms of their own daily lives—that is, lawyers as lawyers, engineers as engineers, politicians as politicians, housewives as housewives, journalists as journalists—about the relevance of the Christian faith to the problems of their normal vocations.

Typical is the question raised by conscientious lawyers: is the state the only source of law or can a judge appeal to some higher code? Similar questions of ultimate profundity have engaged the schoolteachers, the farmers, and the industrialists, who under the Nazi regime and again today are being confronted with serious dilemmas involving personal decisions of far-reaching importance to world peace.

Literally thousands of people in almost all walks of life have been reached within a few years by a dozen academies located at places like Bad Boll, Hermannsburg, Tutzing, Herrenalb, and also in the East Zone. They draw puzzled and distracted people away for a while into a quiet place, to take stock of themselves and their lives in the light of the Christian gospel.

SUFFER THE LITTLE CHILDREN

Of decisive importance for the future of the Christian faith in Germany is the specialized training of catechists in the East Zone to provide regular religious instruction for all children. The war-ravaged church in the Communist orbit was faced with the problem of continuing the Christian education of hundreds of thousands of children after religion was banned from the public schools. Catechetical institutes were quickly organized to train up to 15,000 new teachers to assist the pastors with this gigantic task. Among the 16 million Protestants in the German Democratic Republic are nearly 2 million children and today more than 85 per cent of them are enrolled in these Christian classes! Most of the expense of this program has been borne by the parents and other church members out of regular levies or special contributions, although important gifts from abroad have helped to finance it.

In the province of Thuringia alone 220,000 children are enlisted but 30,000 others remain without teachers. In Berlin today there are 800 full-time catechists, 400 part-time teachers and 300 pastors, organists, and other church workers recruited to provide regular, intensive instruction for 325,000 children (out of 450,000 in the city). In Brandenburg, the province around Berlin with a population of 2,600,000, up to 100 per cent of all children are enrolled in courses under 1,000 Christian leaders! Thus, it may easily be seen that the question of lay training in Germany today is not merely a matter of trying to strengthen the local parish by the addition of a few more interested members but of evangelizing the whole nation to gird it against the onslaught of a non-Christian gospel.

It is a generally recognized fact that school instruction in religion, to which virtually every child in Europe has been exposed for many decades, has failed to prevent the progressive de-christianization of the continent. Many churchmen have strong reservations about the desirability of keeping religious education in the public schools, but they are reluctant to drop it, especially if there seems to be an opportunity to convert it successfully into positive Christian indoctrination.

In most countries, the churches are busily improving the quality of the Sunday school programs, catechetical instruction, and summer camp schedules. As a result of successful experiments in the areas of northern Finnmark where the people are widely scattered, Bishop Smemo of Norway has proposed that large groups of confirmands should be brought together in camps for periods of three to four weeks of concentrated indoctrination. That would be a new kind of concentration camp! But, another problem is presented by the post-confirmation period, when most European youngsters promptly bid farewell to the church just as though they were graduating from a school. Efforts are being made to include the teen-aged boys and girls in special "youth parishes," supervised by full-time youth pastors.

EASTWARD IN EUROPE

It is realized that international movements of all political complexions are competing for the attention of European youth, who—if not firmly grounded in the Christian faith—will inevitably veer and turn with every ideological wind that blows. As matters now stand in Western Europe, the churches in most countries are barely holding their own. This seems to be true of secular youth organizations, too, except that in East Germany all students are impressed into the Free German Youth Movement with remarkable rapidity. Out of 600 students at Leipzig University in mid-1950, there were 80 who had not yielded to the pressure, but by early 1951 only three were left and these were not given work permits in Saxony. Yet 300 attended weekly Bible classes! The presence of good student chaplains in the university centers is of crucial importance.

Evidences of new life are also to be seen in the Orthodox churches of Eastern Europe. It is difficult to assess what is happening in the satellite states because of the scarcity of reliable and objective information regarding significant prewar revival movements such as the Army of the Lord in Rumania. However, the steady growth of Christian lay activity in Greece seems destined to transform the whole Greek Church in the direction of social service and the whole nation toward a new Christian view of life. Right after the war, over 200 leading professional men signed a common declaration of faith in Christian values as the basis of all life.

The core of this lay activity is the Zoe (Life) Movement, which really began about 50 years ago in the popular preaching of Eusebius Mathopoulos. One of its most successful aspects is the publication of the magazine *Zoe,* which has 150,000 subscribers, as well as large editions of popular religious books and Bibles. The Zoe Brotherhood is responsible for 1,500 Sunday schools for 150,000 children and the training of Christian leaders in the church. In order to devote themselves fully to these evangelistic tasks, the members of the brotherhood renounce high offices in the church, accept no remuneration for their work, and do not marry, but live a communal life. They are bound by no onerous rules, however, and may leave the movement when they so desire.

As invariably happens, one inspired movement has inspired others. Today there is a Union of Collaborating Christian Associations, of which Zoe is the senior member. A women's group, named Eussevia, of 6,000 members, is also very active. There is a Young People's Union that has 200 branches and conducts 350 Sunday schools in the Athens area. There is a Student Movement, too. But one of the most remarkable elements in this vital program of Christian revival is Aktines (rays) that was founded in 1937 and concentrates on evangelism of the intelligentsia. Its motto: "If Christ is not the whole reality to all of us, then he is nothing." It is this group that was responsible for the above-mentioned declaration of faith signed by 220 professional leaders in 1946, which was followed up by a Christian Manifesto that raised a storm of angry attack from Communist circles. The general secretary of the Greek Communist Party is reported to have delivered a violent three-hour lecture to his minions for "having slept like foolish virgins whilst our enemies were undermining the very foundations of our party's subsistence."

The practical effect of all this work is already to be seen in the energetic role that certain bishops and parish priests have played in the reconstruction of Northern Greece since the end of the civil war. New life—as in Hungary—bubbles up not out of sheer activism but out of the deeper wells of Biblical study and love for the church.

More than 600 Greek Orthodox priests were killed in World

War II and its aftermath, so that nearly 400 parishes are vacant today. In the summer of 1951 fifty priests from Athens went two-by-two from village to village to minister to the neglected people.

LO, THE FIELDS ARE WHITE

In summing up these all-too-few observations regarding the signs of new life in Christian Europe, two or three general conclusions are worth noting.

The first is that postwar evangelism is definitely concerned with the spiritual problems inside, not outside the continent. In other words, it is for the present at least directing its energies less toward winning the whole world for Christ than toward *winning one's neighborhood for Christ*. This is noteworthy because it is always easier for people (including Americans!) to see an opportunity for missionary witness at a distance than to discern it close at hand. This does not mean that European interest in foreign missions is dying. As we have already seen, heroic efforts are being made to resume support of the enterprises in far-flung fields that had been maintained by the continental societies. Money and men are once more being sent out to Asia and Africa. In the long run, these large foreign enterprises of the European churches tend to gain by the vast mission program that must be undertaken right at home!

Secondly, evangelism is being recognized in many places as the principal and primary *task of established religion,* not only of the so-called free churches and the peripheral sects. Theoretically, the regular revival of religion on the parish level was always a part of the church program, but the fact that it was associated with the inner mission psychology—reviving the lapsed rather than saving the lost—usually deprived evangelistic campaigns of their elementary missionary force. Besides, the Inner Mission Movement itself stood outside the formal church structure.

As long as the pastors themselves did not regard Europe as a mission field, it was inevitable that the more aggressive American and British evangelistic movements would do so. This was resented as proselytism, sometimes quite rightly but sometimes quite wrongly. Since the end of World War II the so-called gospel sects have intensified their activity, but it seems safe to say that the renewal of Christian life within the older churches, such as I have described, holds out far more promise for the re-Christianization of Europe than the preaching of the self-styled faith missions, or the promotion of any particular spiritual discipline such as Moral Rearmament. Nevertheless the indirect influence of these predominantly American groups, including Jehovah's Witnesses, Youth for Christ, Mormons, and others, cannot be denied.

Thirdly, the most characteristic thing that can be said about the new evangelism in Europe is that—in contrast to much of the revivalism of the past century—it is centered in a new search for Christian fellowship on the broad basis of *community-wide regeneration*. Individual salvation has little appeal for the European of today, who often feels less need of coming to peace with his God than of finding peace in his world. Perhaps this is the major reason for the failure of time-hallowed revival methods that aimed, first of all, to give peace of heart and mind to the individual regardless of the state of the world around him. In these days man and his world have become one. The mind of the average European, no matter what part of the continent he inhabits, is full of problems that loom larger than his own salvation.

Before proceeding to a discussion of specific issues and areas in Europe, it is necessary to get to know the average European a little better, to take a sweeping view of the whole continent, and to fix in our minds the relationship of geographic, political, and religious influences that affect the deepest levels of its life.

3

Can Europe Ever Be Unified?

It is the common tradition of Christianity that has made Europe what it is.—The Bishop of Chichester.

The life and death question for Europe is, then, whether it can rediscover its own specific mission.—Dr. W. A. Visser 't Hooft.

EUROPE as a place name was once confined to a very small stretch of the Balkans north of ancient Greece. Herodotus, the first great historian, had no idea of the true size of the unexplored European continent. He reported that the Persian Army had marched "through Europe" on the way from the Hellespont to Athens. By the same logic, the same army traversing a coastal strip near Carthage would have crossed what was then known as Africa! But the name Asia had a similar small beginning. Indeed, all three great continents first found their names around the eastern end of the Mediterranean. Then—like the sons of Noah who after the great flood sired the three races that peopled the world—these insignificant place names gradually spread over vast land masses. Europe was destined to be the smallest but the most explosive of them all.

The name Europe, according to some scholars, is derived from a Greek combination signifying "dark countenance," referring perhaps to the black soil of Macedonia. Others point to Assyrian inscriptions wherein Ereb (land of the setting sun) is distinguished from Asu (land of the rising sun). Merchants of Phoenicia—from whose shores, incidentally, a legendary beauty named Europa was enticed westward by Zeus in the form of a white bull—brought both expressions to Greece and thus the two continents were first identified. Something of the fate of Europe lingers in both of these explanations. Europa is the child of Asia in the same sense that America is the child of Europe.

Despite the early distinction between the two continents, the exact boundary between Europe and Asia has never been drawn, at least on land. Why—in the wisdom of God—was an ocean not fixed between them? At least some of the subsequent bloodshed might have been averted. The older geographies describe modern Europe as extending east to the Urals and South to the Caucasus, thus including European Russia. But today all distinctions between European Russia and Asiatic Russia have disappeared from the map. Indeed, there is a general inclination to assume that Asia itself has moved west to the Elbe in Germany. Is this an accurate description of the return of communism toward the West that gave it birth? If so, the riddle of the future is: will Asia some day reach the English Channel? Then Europe, considered as a separate geographical entity, would simply disappear.

There have been other times in history—long before the advent of the USSR—when it seemed as though the boundary between East and West might be erased, but subjection by force has never proved permanent. Huns and Turks have swept westward; Germans, Swedes, and French have swept eastward. For centuries it seemed as though the Christian church might prove to be the binding element that would weld the two worlds together, but in 1054 the arrogance and political ambitions of the Roman Pope in presuming to excommunicate the Patriarch of Constantinople brought about the first great split in Christendom. It is no exaggeration to say that much of our modern trouble can be laid to this unhappy division between the Christian East and the Christian West nearly ten centuries ago. The lines of that division between the Orthodox and Roman Catholic churches are still to be found in the line of partition that splits Europe today. (See Chapter Seven.)

THE HUBBUB OF THE UNIVERSE

Geographically, Europe has often been belittled as nothing more than a peninsula of Asia, which for haphazard historical reasons has been granted a continental status it hardly deserves. The fact is that this important promontory has been the pivot around which all our history revolves. There was a recent tendency, up to about 1950, to assume that Europe's role as a pivotal power was ended—especially with the decline of Britain as a world power—and that either North America or Soviet Asia would run the world or cut it in half. Shortly after the outbreak of the Korean War this tide of thought began to turn again. Let's take a brief glance at the reasons for this.

For one thing, Europe is still the main crossroads of the world's commerce. It will be remembered that Palestine in Old Testament times occupied a strategic position between great powers, giving Israel a degree of importance out of all proportion to its size. The same thing, geographically, is true of Europe. For instance, it is situated well in the center of the Northern Hemisphere, which contains 80 per cent of the world's land. Today, more than ever, all Europe has become the buffer area between new East and new West.

For another thing, Europe is the acknowledged birthplace of our culture and the cradle of our Western civilization. She is the successor to ancient Greece and ancient Rome, the center of civilization having moved slightly north and west from the Mediterranean after the global discoveries of the fifteenth and sixteenth centuries. For many generations Europeans have developed and governed the seas and the land. For a high level of intelligence and ability they still rival or outrank the rest of the world.

Moreover, the very fact that two great non-European powers are contending for world supremacy has given Europe a new lease on life. The theater of war has shifted to East Asia, but the real center of the struggle, and the theater of interest, stays in Europe. Have not Europe's recovery and return to prominence been hastened by the conflicts in Korea and Indo-China? Pride, prestige, and self-respect are being restored to many European countries, including Western Germany, in the headlong race for allies. Early in 1952, the Bonn government regained virtual independence in return for military participation in a Western defense plan! Meanwhile the Russian Zone had been set up as an independent German Democratic Republic. This is certainly the worst result of the tug of war in Europe: namely, that the whole peninsula has been torn in half. The USSR has almost but not quite swallowed Vienna and Berlin. Although only half of Europe remains outside the Russian orbit, it is nonetheless true that the amputated peninsula—Western Europe—looms as large as ever in world affairs, if only as a bone of contention. But it is much more than that.

Battered though she is, Europe is potentially an economic, political, cultural, and spiritual powerhouse. Here is still the greatest import-export market of the world, the breeding place of every modern political philosophy, the natural home of music and art, and the chief arena of the conflict between Christ and militant atheism. Europe's capacity to control the course of world events remains almost unimpaired. Europe remains Europe!

It is also a powderhouse. World War II was fought primarily to break the power of one man over Europe and to destroy his ideology. The military mission was successfully accomplished to the accompaniment of tremendous physical destruction and suffering. Hitler was annihilated, but it may be argued that the effort to eradicate the fascist philosophy in Central Europe and replace it with genuine democratic ideals was never seriously attempted. Fascism is publicly discredited, yes, but so is democracy in many quarters. The bruised and bleeding continent has plenty of guides but no direction, and in the short space of six years they have taken Europe three-quarters of the way around—not away from—another war.

FUMBLING WITH DEMOCRACY

Postwar history at this point may be telescoped as follows: first, the purging process (1945-46); second, economic reconstruction (1947-49); third, military rearmament (1950-?). The fact that this list unfortunately does not include spiritual revival is noteworthy. There was not time for that. The given dates only roughly approximate the high tide of each stage (even for Germany) and are used merely to illustrate the extreme brevity of the first two stages.

It may be argued that the period of purge was inspired by the low motives of the Morgenthau Plan, which fortunately was never really carried into execution; or by the high tone of Justice Jackson's opening address at the Nuremberg trials, which cannot be said to have achieved their purpose. But the fact to remember is that the swift evolution within each stage, to say nothing of the headlong progress toward the next stage, was dictated by the apparently irresistible pressure of external and alien events.

It was a dictated purge, a dictated rehabilitation, and a dictated rearmament—dictated, to be sure, by overpowering circumstances rather than by the tyrannical desire of any one man to impose his will on another. Europe moved along like a figure in a Greek tragedy. Democracy, which Archbishop William Temple called "a definitely Christian product," never had a real chance. The Russians were completely totalitarian in placing the stamp of Soviet state socialism on the so-called "peoples' democracies" in Eastern Europe, thus bringing a word that had never enjoyed great respect in Central Europe into complete disrepute. On the other hand, the American version of democracy was launched by the most undemocratic of all agencies: namely, the armed forces, in an economic situation that had to be sustained by all sorts of financial transfusions. These were prescribed largely—except for voluntary relief and reconstruction activities—by self-interest, sometimes enlightened, sometimes not.

Then, in the spring of 1948, came the start of the Cold War, which inevitably launched a rearmament race. Peaceful plans for putting Europe back on her feet were bound, under the tragic circumstances, to be transformed into plans for putting her back in arms. Could any of this, even by the most liberal employment of the term, be characterized as the result of a democratic process? The inevitable question is, "Well, what else could be done?" The best counter-question is: "Was anything else seriously attempted?"

The ultimate effect of this complete reversal of purposes is that total destruction and unconditional surrender are in danger of being replaced by total recovery! In such a context total recovery does not have a pleasant sound, because it implies the restoration of much that should remain rubble. Economic assets immediately become military resources and men nothing more than manpower.

Above all, you cannot consistently spend three years discouraging the idea of war and the next three years forcing preparations for another one without doing violence to the very souls of men. The

United States sincerely believes that the whole world is in great danger from Communist Russia, and there is little reason to doubt that the conquest of the world is the Soviet aim. Russia, on the other hand, ostensibly believes that the whole world is in great danger from the capitalist United States. Between the two—whether she likes it or not—Europe is already being prepared for another total war! Whether the vicious circle can eventually be broken may depend wholly on the churches that we have set out to study.

DIVIDED THEY STAND!

In the midst of all this, the intelligent European occupies a mental position that is frequently difficult for a non-European to comprehend. For one thing, he seems to us unreasonably cool. People inhabiting the slopes of a volcanic island do not bolt at every wisp of smoke; they know the risk they run, take what precautions they can, but regard occasional disasters as inevitable. And they have a better sense of history. I remember my own incredulous amazement when in the early 1930's some Europeans informed me calmly that the United States and Japan would soon be at war. To my unpracticed eye there did not seem a cloud in the sky, but to the European mind the clash between expanding interests could only issue in a desperate battle. This accounts for the European assumption that war between the USSR and the USA will come sooner or later, and also for the remarkable lack of nervousness they display at every preliminary skirmish between the sparring giants despite the genuine horror they feel at the thought of being caught in the middle.

The average European is a combination of many other characteristics that give him his distinctive continental personality. He is mature and worldly-wise, less likely than Americans to be swept away by sudden gusts of violent emotion raised by "world problems." While more tolerant of human foibles and failings, he is susceptible to strong social prejudices and an acute class consciousness. We Americans glory in our "rugged individualism" but in practically every respect, save our lack of reverence for precedent, the Europeans are far more individualistic than we are. We pursue a way of life; they cultivate an art of living. Two American characteristics are sufficiently pronounced to have become a particular source of quiet amusement or vexation to the European who is content to make his peace with each passing day: namely, our burning haste to establish Utopia now; and our bland assumption that it is up to us to see that it gets done.

Europe, in other words, is sophisticated. This sophistication is neither good nor bad in itself, but, like a neutral polish, impersonally appears on her manners, her philosophies, and also on her religious convictions. Good or evil must be sought below the sophisticated surface.

Existentialism is the most popular polish at the present time. There are many kinds of existentialism (Sartre being merely the most sensational exponent of one brand) but all of it begins with what "exists." It is a desperate and sincere effort to be realistic in a day of punctured illusions and ruptured ideological systems, and it is probably better than nothing.

Great numbers of well educated Europeans, despite religious statistics, are completely innocent of any vital philosophy or religious convictions, while others have depths of faith that relatively few church-going Americans can even appreciate, because our faith has never been tested as theirs has. The struggle for the soul of Europe will probably be decided by the ability of the kind of Christian faith experienced by these latter individuals to propagate itself. It is the precious possession of a very small minority today, as we shall shortly see.

PUSHED INTO PULLING TOGETHER

The emergence of two non-European world powers has done at least one very good thing for Europe: it has, despite the split between East and West, begun to unify it. Individualism had been carried too far, and there had been no counteracting passion for unity such as the United States has known as a result of the two great struggles that in 1776 and 1861 formed and reformed the nation. Wars in Europe have unified nations but always served to re-divide the continent. Whereas the basic American motto is: "United we stand, divided we fall," it might almost be said that European balance-of-power policy was: "Divided we stand, united we fall." Slowly but steadily that philosophy is being superseded by the stark reality that, if she does not hold together now, imperial Europe is slated to become a cluster of American or Russian dependencies. Competition with the two huge economies of the East and the West is possible only if Europe unites.

The desire for a United Europe has been accelerated by fear of Russia and by fear of the United States. These fears, of course, have become most vocal and visible in Western Europe, where the four freedoms are far from being a dead letter. Understandably enough, Europeans would rather live their own lives. To do so they realize that they must be strong. Sufficient strength can be generated only by the pooling of all resources. Up to this point, United States policy fully supports the European unionists and is not greatly disturbed by the fact that fear of America is one of the most impelling factors toward union. Beyond this point, however, the roads tend to divide. A few outspoken Western Europeans whole-heartedly support a full alliance with the United States, even to war against Russia, while a great many others—to put it mildly—would rather not commit themselves.

As yet, happily, there is no real reason to fear that Austria is being irreparably sawn asunder as the result of her present separation into two major zones. The same cannot be said about Germany. But even if the immediate effect of the Iron Curtain is to set up two Europes instead of one, their affinity for each other will probably continue to be greater than any non-European powers can overcome. This strong centripetal force is especially evident in Germany right now. There is even reason to hope that a real European union would exercise a powerful pull on the vassal states of the USSR. History clearly indicates that all efforts to drive outside wedges into the European peoples have sooner or later provoked violent reaction. This reaction manifested itself again when Europe awoke to the fact of its being partitioned between the United States and the USSR.

MILITANT NEUTRALITY IS NEGATIVE

The idea of neutrality plays an important role in Western European thought today. The peak of its popularity passed in 1951 when the shift from economic recovery to rearmament was being publicly debated.[1] Nobody wanted it, but by the beginning of 1952 rearmament, except perhaps in Germany, was a generally accepted fact. The European army under General Eisenhower had become a fighting force and ECA had been replaced without further ado by the Mutual Security Agency, which subordinated peaceful reconstruc-

---

[1] As one Frenchman expressed it in a widely-read article entitled "Neutralism" in the spring of 1951, "Between the prospect of slavery to Moscow and that of a war which could mean suicide, a large section of European opinion looks instructively for a third alternative. People are aware that without the friendship, the help, the power of America, they would have been crushed long ago [but they] don't want to give up all hope of the establishment of an equilibrium of mutual concessions between a liberal capitalism which embarks on social enterprises under government authority like that of Tennessee Valley . . . and a socialism which in the nature of things will be compelled one day to recognize the value of liberty."

tion to military defense. The realistic European was aware that the Rubicon of neutrality had already been crossed. Nevertheless, "neutralism" persisted as an active factor in the minds of Europeans who struggle for a respectable middle position in the East-West conflict. What many of them have in mind is not so much passive resistance or conscientious objection as it is a "third force"—like the armed neutrality of Switzerland or Sweden—that might even grow strong enough to bring the two giants to terms and prevent another conflict.

Except for some firebrand revisionists in the West and the war mentality of desperate anti-Communists in the East, Europe genuinely wants peace. Here is the crucial point. If neutrality is to have a decisive and positive effect, exactly what is Europe's role to be? It is not enough to say with lifted eyes—as some Europeans do— that Europe has a sacred mission of her own. What *is* the mission? This question has not yet been answered. Is it merely a matter of salvaging the European art of living? Definitely not. Is it merely opposition to both Russia and the USA? That is too negative.

Christian thinkers like to hold out the hope that Europe will once more represent those Christian values that Russia has thrown overboard and that the United States—they think—is in great danger of forgetting because of its new preeminence in the world. They fully realize that Europe must first re-win them for herself, but they believe that St. Paul's response to the cry from Macedonia, instead of going into Asia, gives Europe a special place in the divine economy. As one theologian puts it, the road taken by the church of Christ across Europe endows Europeans with a special place among God's people. A dramatic and dynamic thought! Can it be put to humble work without running the very real risk of turning the European idea into an *ersatz* religion? Some leaders think that the answer is to be found in a European federation.

COOPERATION IS MORE CONSTRUCTIVE

Ever since war's end the European churches have placed heavy stress on the importance of laymen in the church and of Christian men and women witnessing to their faith in the workaday world. This was one of the really good results of wartime opposition to fascism, arising from the discovery that pastors alone were but a feeble foil against rampant persecution. Ultimately a select group of outstanding Protestant laymen of Europe came together in what was called the Ecumenical Commission on European Cooperation. In January, 1951, when the question of European cooperation was a burning issue, they had a discussion that issued in a brief informal statement. No program had been launched and no resolutions voted, but here are some significant highlights from the report:

The peoples of Western Europe are at the moment confronted with a new political situation which demands a complete reorientation of the policy which they have been following for the last five years. The main effort in Western Europe during these years has been directed to economic and social rehabilitation, while at the same time definite attempts were being made to achieve closer European cooperation in order to strengthen the political and economic position of Europe in a world of growing tension between East and West. Economic rehabilitation has succeeded in most countries, thanks to American aid. The idea of European cooperation has met with great response in public opinion and some headway has been made in the attempts at unification, the most interesting of which is embodied in the Schuman Plan. All this work of rehabilitation and political unification was conceived of as a long-term effort, in which full consideration was given to the financial implications and the economic and social repercussions.

In the last few months the pace of history has changed.[1] Europe is now confronted with a growing fear that showdown between the Western powers and the Soviet Union is imminent, so that we find our-

[1] Referring, no doubt, to the outbreak of the Korean war in June, 1950.

selves . . . in a period of great tension which may lead to war. . . .
While in the USA, Government, Congress, and public opinion are con-
centrating on preparations for the emergency and are making great
efforts to strengthen their position on a global scale, most of the peoples
of Europe are very reluctant to change the priorities in their domestic
policies, and to subordinate everything to rearmament. . . . The USA
is aware of the gravity of developments on a world level, but it under-
rates the dilemma in which European countries are placed, as they have
at the same time to maintain their economic and social equilibrium and
to build up military defense. . . .

For all these reasons the idea of neutrality finds today a great deal
of popular support, although many people are aware that for Europe
to be neutral and independent in the modern world implies some form
of political and military unification. . . . So far the idea of the political
unification of Europe has been a long-term proposition. . . . Would
European cooperation be of any help in the solving of today's problems?
We believe that this is indeed the case. . . . The situation represents a
challenge to European churches. For as has become clear from the foregoing, the question of European unity is not merely a tactical political
problem, but . . . a moral and spiritual issue of decisive importance.

From these excerpts it is apparent that European Christians have
not only an astonishing feeling of continental loyalty that is more
than solidarity, but also a strong sense of Christian responsibility.
They are more interested in constructive cooperation than in remilitarization. Europe in their minds represents much more than a
potential economic or political unit and unified military command.
Its unity must be erected on a spiritual rock, not a common defense project.

WHAT CAN THE CHURCHES CONTRIBUTE?

The rearmament of Europe began with a survey of resources.
The re-Christianization of Europe can begin there, too. Every postwar military establishment includes guns that won't shoot and

planes that cannot fly. The churches of Europe, as elsewhere, are similarly equipped with armies that won't march. For all statistical purposes the population of old Europe—up to the Russian frontier —is a nominally Christian population. The number of Jews, Moslems, atheists, and others outside the Christian church has always been small, and today, since Hitler's attempt to exterminate the Jews, very small indeed. But official census figures take no account of *active* church membership. The churches themselves usually accept the governmental tabulations, even while acknowledging that such totals do not really reflect the religious strength of the nation.

By and large, the population of Europe (excluding Russia) is upwards of 360 million, of whom approximately 200 million are Roman Catholic, 120 million are Protestant, and 25 million are Orthodox.

The Roman Catholics are located principally in the southern or Latin countries stretching from Spain (27 million) and Portugal, through France (40 million), to Italy (45 million), but reach northward into England (Ireland, of course), Holland, Germany (20 million), Poland, and Lithuania, as well as down into the Danube through Austria and Hungary to Rumania. Protestants predominate in Northern Europe beginning in Great Britain (40 million) and proceeding through Holland, Germany (40 million), Denmark, Norway, Sweden, Finland, Estonia, and Latvia, but also touching the southern nations. The Orthodox are situated almost exclusively, except for refugees, in Eastern Europe, chiefly on the Balkan peninsula in Rumania, Bulgaria, Yugoslavia, and Greece.

Within the Protestant fellowship, the most numerous are the Lutherans, who total about 65 million on the continent, some of whom are in the "evangelical" union churches of North Germany. The principal Lutheran areas are Scandinavia (Denmark, Norway,

Sweden, and Finland are nearly 100 per cent Lutheran) and Germany (nearly 40 million). West Germany, incidentally, had a population of 47,600,000 in 1950, of whom 50 per cent were Protestant and 45.2 per cent Catholic. East Germany is predominantly Protestant.

The Anglicans, who sometimes protest against being numbered among the Protestants, count 27 million members in England (60 per cent of all babies are baptized into the Church of England), but list only 3 million on the "electoral" roll as a better reflection of active membership.

The Reformed churches of Europe number about 15 million members, and occupy a predominant position in Scotland, Holland, and Switzerland, as well as being the strongest Protestant element in countries like France and Hungary.[1] All other Protestant groups taken together would not number more than a few million and not one of them can be said to have laid the stamp of its genius upon any European nation.

The Methodists are approximately one million, having nearly 800,000 members in Great Britain, where the movement took its start. The Baptists in 1951 counted almost 600,000 registered members, not including their membership in European Russia, which—with an estimated 2 million adherents—is the only considerable Protestant factor in the USSR today. Congregationalists are to be found principally in Great Britain, and they total about 500,000 altogether. Of special interest because of their full membership in the World Council of Churches are the Old Catholics, who number about 400,000 members in Europe and, like the Anglicans, think of themselves as a possible bridge to bring Roman Catholics and Protestants together again.

[1] Under Reformed churches are grouped all bodies variously described as Calvinist or Presbyterian. In Europe they are generally labeled Reformed.

THE TEST OF GIDEON

From the standpoint of the real status of the Christian faith, the statistics of the smaller communions are a far more accurate index of active membership than the impressive totals of the big churches. Europe is not as Christian as the figures seem to indicate.

This is true, first of all, of the Roman Catholic Church. At least one Italian bishop admits that only 10 per cent of his Italian population are practicing Roman Catholics; a few years ago the Communist following was almost as numerous. As regards France, there may be about 40 million baptized Roman Catholics, but not even the Roman Church counts more than 6 million members who are active. Regardless of the fact that French Catholics have been foremost in carrying the missionary flag into every corner of the world, we can only conclude this enumeration by subtracting 34 million from the Roman Catholic world membership of 400 million, which with a similar subtraction in Italy runs to one-fifth of the total!

Lutheran statistics can be just as deceptive. The Scandinavian pastors regularly confess that not more than one-tenth of the average parish betrays any lively interest in the church. Frequently, the interest of this 10 per cent begins and ends with attendance at one Communion service per year. Whereas only one per cent of Norwegian young people in a 1952 poll openly registered their hostility to the Christian religion, 60 per cent said they were not much interested. This occurred in an area where church loyalty is above average: 14 per cent of the 680 teen-agers declared themselves to be Christians and 25 per cent said they were well-disposed toward the Christian faith.

In England at Easter, 1947, it was computed that 6 million persons out of the 37 million population went to Communion: namely, nearly all of the Roman Catholics (2 million out of 3 million), very few of the Anglicans (2 million out of 27 million), and about 2 million out of the 6 million members belonging to all other denominations. Much the same sad picture prevails, for example, among the Reformed in Switzerland.

The religious and political picture of Europe, as presented here, is not very reassuring. If a modern Gideon were to summon all the Christians of Europe to battle, he would be forced to begin—even before the elimination of those who would inevitably lie down comfortably to quench their thirst—with a 90 per cent cut in his nominal rolls. This alone would reduce his Christian cohorts from about 350 million to 35 million souls, which in turn are subdivided into four major confessional groups and a bewildering array of smaller loyalties.

This lack of unity is disheartening, but it need not prove fatal. Even with split forces the war against atheistic communism can be won, provided that it is waged on a spiritual, not a political, level. For, although we may deplore the divisions that rend the church, it is invariably true that the Christian witness is most effective and church life is most active wherever competition is keenest.

Perhaps competition is not a pleasant word, but it is an honest one. In Europe, for example, a rough line of demarcation between the Roman Catholic south and the Protestant north runs right through Holland, Germany, and Czechoslovakia, although Poland to the north is almost wholly Catholic. But it is along this axis, on the average, that the most vigorous and well developed church life is to be found, as well as the closest working relationship between the various confessions.

Even in these countries, however, the unwieldy memberships based on baptized populations suffer from their own excessive weight. There are not enough pastors for the people. Compare, if you will, the vitality of the relatively small free church congregations in Europe or the United States with their bigger and older sister parishes, not only in terms of financial support but in terms of personal fellowship, regular worship, neighborhood evangelism, Christian education of the youth, and the participation of laymen in all phases of the work!

FIRST OBJECTIVE: CHANGE THE CHURCH!

The inability of the church to make its full contribution toward the unity of Europe does not rest so much in the diversity of creeds and political preferences as in what might be called a neutral or non-committal attitude toward man. Centuries of social stratification had produced a religion that combines great confidence in the providence of God with a fundamental skepticism regarding the essential equality of men. The church invariably found itself defending the social *status quo* and avoiding the hazards of change that might adversely affect its own position. Roman Catholicism, Anglicanism, Lutheranism, and, to a somewhat lesser degree, Calvinism, have all clearly given evidence of this attitude, especially in Europe.

This attitude helps to account for the relatively slow growth of political democracy in most European states. With all its faults, American democracy is firmly based: first, on a sense of the *dignity* of each individual; and, second, on an insistence upon the rights and privileges of personal *responsibility* in community affairs. The church in the United States and Canada has not only contributed much to the evolution of this political faith but derived much from it, and therefore—despite the separation of church and state—the link between religious and political convictions in these countries is remarkably strong. American Protestantism's great danger, of course, lies not so much in reactionary conservatism, though there is plenty of that, but in substituting faith in man's productiveness for faith in God's providence.

The wide gap between religion and politics in Europe is exceedingly serious, because it leaves a vacuum that can be filled only by pseudo-religious ideologies such as fascism and communism. Too many Europeans, as matters now stand, pray according to their religious creed but vote according to an ideology, thus revealing an Iron Curtain within themselves. Not only Europe, but the average European, is torn in half. He is not necessarily Communist, but he is certainly no more than half Christian.

Four hundred years ago the Protestant Reformation—and subsequently the Roman Counter-Reformation—effectively filled the empty shell of the Holy Roman Empire at a time when it was under attack from Islam. This was achieved, not by calling for a crusade against the Turks who were besieging Vienna, but by changing the church. Today the spiritual impulse of that great religious revolution seems to have died away, leaving only a thin trickle of ineffective revivals. A crusade against communism will not cure this condition, which requires nothing less than another great conversion to bring the church abreast of our times. The sober question confronting Christianity today, therefore, is this: does it contain the fresh reserves of power that are required in order to give shape and substance to Europe—and to the world—for the next four hundred years?

4

The Need For a New Society

The proof of our ability to lead Christian lives is not to be discovered only in our devotional exercises, but rather in the extent to which we as individuals can move the society wherein we live to employ Christian methods and standards.
—*Sir Stafford Cripps.*

FOR nineteen centuries the story of the Good Samaritan, the simple admonitions about giving a cup of cold water and visiting the prisoner, as well as Jesus' healing of the blind and the lame, have turned Christians in every generation to similar deeds of mercy. To say, as some do, that the church has had no social conscience is ridiculous. Never has there been a time when the Christian church in all of its parts has not given evidence of a strong sense of responsibility toward society.

It is true that its response to social needs has sometimes been tardy and inadequate, and still is. It is also true that occasionally its response may have been temporarily misguided into justifying evils such as child labor, human slavery, or the incarceration of debtors. But who can deny that when the time came for sweeping away these abuses it was the Christian conscience that wielded the broom?

Thus, for hundreds of years before the word socialism was even coined, Christian agencies were ministering to the sick, harboring the aged, educating the ignorant, relieving the oppressed, feeding the poor, and, in general, making the world a better place to live in. *This was and is social service.* In the Middle Ages, Europe was already dotted with orphanages, asylums, pest houses, hostelries, and other establishments for social service.

Relics of these ancient foundations are still visible: the kennels of the Swiss monastery of St. Bernard in the high Alps (fifth century), the shelters erected by Knights Hospitaler of St. John (medical corps of the Crusades), the quaint *béguinages* of Belgium (thirteenth century) and the Fugger homes in Augsburg (sixteenth century), to say nothing of the great university centers of learning like Paris and Oxford. No cold and calculated plan of social betterment produced these institutions. They were the fruit of Jesus' command to his followers, "Love one another."

To be sure, there were major and minor changes in the nature of social service during the long course of the centuries. The simple sharing of the first Christians gave way in time to a mechanical accounting system whereby good works were certified by the church to pay spiritual dividends. Christian charity has had difficulty ever since, trying to dissociate itself from the uncharitable notion that it was deliberately designed to render a greater blessing to the benefactor than to the beneficiary.

During the later Middle Ages, when all Europe became nominally Christian and was dominated by the Roman Church, great monasteries and religious orders sprang up and became the natural centers of social service, thus relieving individuals and local congregations of much of their responsibility. Into their swollen coffers flowed the gifts of the pious and the conscience-stricken. Never has the splendid concept of storing up treasure in heaven been so grossly distorted.

The Reformation was, in part, sustained by a popular revolt

against ecclesiastical wealth. It resulted not only in the confiscation of much church property but also in the transfer of communal matters such as public health and general welfare, including education, into the hands of the civil government, which was at that time avowedly Christian. That did not mean that the church had thereby washed its hands of any one of these public problems, but rather it expressed the novel and democratic idea that such things were a legitimate public charge that should be placed under public supervision rather than conducted as a semi-private enterprise of the church.

THE CHRISTIAN SOCIAL IMPERATIVE

In the light of the present-day distinction between church and state, this sixteenth century transfer of social welfare to the civil government can be seen as the origin of secular social service. Totalitarian states of the twentieth century—greedier than the medieval church—have cold-bloodedly attempted to complete the process by driving the church completely out of the domain of public welfare. It is indicative of the importance that European churches attach to their social work that they regarded such encroachments as attacks against the very fabric of Christian life. Gentle Pastor Von Bodelschwingh, head of the great community of charitable institutions at Bethel-Bielefeld, barred with his body the efforts of the Nazis to remove deformed children from his institution in order to exterminate them.

All over Western Europe Christian social service has taken a new lease on life since the war because of a new appreciation by the church of its responsibility to society—a responsibility that the state cannot possibly fulfill. But it cannot be affirmed that the social sciences as a whole are equally interested in reserving a place for Christian participation in the field of public welfare. All too frequently the church is patiently humored like a well intentioned old lady who is likely to raise a fuss when crossed.

Historically, this is not difficult to understand. By and large the social interests of all European churches have followed the usual unexciting pattern of parish welfare, admonitions regarding national morality, and gestures of international brotherhood.

Differences from country to country, if any, are to be found chiefly in varieties of approach rather than in the problems themselves; the Germans usually beginning with a scientific analysis of the theories about a given situation, the French with considerable doubt about being able to alter human nature anyway, and the British with the deceptively casual air of not really meaning to make any substantial changes at all. Everywhere you find the same committees or commissions on sex and family, education, temperance, public morals, and so on. Everywhere are kindergartens, prison chaplains, seamen's missions, and watch-dog delegations appointed to keep a careful eye on the burning issues of the moment. Not long ago the Stockholm City Mission (in socialist Sweden!) revealed an impressive list of activities that began a century ago with Sunday schools and day schools for children but have since developed into services that reach out to apprentices, liberated prisoners, wayward girls, and alcoholics! This is work that must be done and for which society is grateful to Christianity, but today it is no longer enough.

WESTERN EUROPE'S POSTWAR PLIGHT

It is impossible in one brief volume to deal with social issues in every part of Europe. This discussion must therefore be limited almost entirely to Great Britain, with occasional references to France, and a passing glance at Belgium and Holland. The reasons for using these four West European nations are rather obvious. They have certain striking similarities despite equally great disparities.

In general, this is their situation: They all belong to the victor states of World War II and, except for Spain and Portugal, are the only colonial powers left in Europe. But this fortunate circumstance has not spared them from suffering the same serious impoverishment as the rest of the war-torn continent. Owing to their flourishing empires, they had built up a disproportionately large and prosperous middle class (civil servants, shopkeepers and others) that was the backbone of European democracy, especially in Britain. The struggle toward greater social security in these seaboard countries has always centered in the middle class, especially in the lower middle class, and not in the proletariat.

Today, owing to the loss of colonial resources, hundreds of thousands of middle class citizens find the ground cut from under them, and they have become not only a national luxury but an economic liability, even though they may still be a political and cultural asset. So critical is their predicament that they are often referred to as "economic" refugees, which is no less disagreeable than becoming a DP.

This development is to be seen most graphically in the return of the Dutch from Indonesia or of the British from India and Western Asia. Somehow they must be reabsorbed in the national economy of their own countries, quite apart from the decision of some of them to emigrate. It is this necessity that has forced every one of the victorious and imperial powers, with its strong democratic traditions, to turn increasingly to some form of modified socialism. Nowhere is this drama more striking than in Britain during recent years.

Another reason for singling out Britain here is that it is a predominantly Protestant and Anglo-Saxon country, which bears a strong family resemblance to the United States and Canada. The resemblance thus carries over to church life itself and aids in revealing the extent of the church's interest in social service and its role in social reform.

The Christian of Britain, as is to be expected, seeks solutions for a wide variety of ordinary social problems with great diligence, through activities ranging on the parish level from Christmas baskets and church sales, to special clinics on marriage problems and family life. On a national level, frontal assaults are mounted against alcoholism and—in latter years—gambling, which in all of its many forms is estimated to attract 72 per cent of the British adult population, although its popularity with the younger people may be waning slightly.[1] It will be remembered that Princess Elizabeth was loudly applauded about a year before her accession, when she delivered a notably stern lecture on morals to her people in a tone that reminded many of Queen Victoria.

To carry this very superficial survey of Christian social interest in Britain onto the world level is to discover a far-reaching and liberal concern for foreign missions and Commonwealth affairs, with special emphasis on specific issues such as the racial tensions in South Africa. Despite postwar poverty, a discreet notice in the advertising columns of *The Times,* regarding some remote but appealing need, is often sufficient to start a substantial flow of contributions.

In view of this widespread interest in social problems, to say nothing of some of the newer approaches described in Chapter Two, it might be thought that the postwar church in Britain would be nationally recognized as a front-rank champion of human rights and social progress. Unfortunately, this is not the case. In fact, there is probably no country in the world where the church has shown it-

---

[1] A recent church commission, after a long investigation of the whole gambling problem, produced a surprisingly tolerant report on this dubious national pastime!

self to be a real pioneer of a better social order. At the end of the war an official Anglican Commission on "The Conversion of England" reported: "There can be no doubt that there is a wide and deep gulf between the church and the people. [There is] a wholesale drift from organized religion." [1]

You do not have to go far to find one of the reasons. Despite the historic interest of the church in public morality and social *service*, only a few of its membership—not the church itself—are to be found in the vanguard of the struggle for social *justice*. What is the difference? Briefly, social service is primarily concerned with acts of mercy, whereas social justice is based on the belief that pious alms are no substitute for human rights.

THE INADEQUACY OF SOCIAL SERVICE

More than thirty years before he became the archbishop of Canterbury, William Temple said, "The social problem does not consist of slums, or of excessive numbers of public houses; these are symptoms and aggravations of the problem, but the problem itself lies deeper." [2] Three reasons might be advanced to account for the fact that the Christian church in Europe—despite all its good works—does not emerge clearly in the forefront of the crusade for social justice. They may also help to explain the excessively hostile attitude evidenced by so many European social reformers toward the church. Above all, they are factors that must be adequately dealt with before the church can regain the leadership it has lost.

The first reason applies to *Christian social service itself, which, as inherited from the nineteenth century, consists almost entirely in*

---

[1] There is also a drift from the ministry. Whereas in 1914 there were 20,000 Anglican parish priests in England, in 1951 there were only 15,000.

[2] *William Temple's Teaching,* by A. E. Baker, p. 157. Philadelphia, Westminster Press, 1951.

acts of charity aimed at helping individuals in distress. The cancers of society are treated as headcolds. The application of Christian first aid (for that is what it amounts to) is not concerned with preventing future distress but largely with alleviating the immediate problems of specific persons in specific situations. First aid is undoubtedly important and there is nothing intrinsically wrong with it, as long as it does not induce a state of permanent dependence in the person who is being helped. Drunkenness, debauchery, dishonesty, and dirt may have a certain fascination for the avid reading public; but at close range they are not agreeable daily companions and somebody must certainly concern himself with them.

Perpetual emergency help, however, is fraught with both spiritual and social peril. Even though it finds firm roots in the unassailable truth that redemption itself is on an individual basis, not by groups, classes, or masses, our best social service generally falls short of being redemptive because it is merely remedial. The average European, despite his desperate need for food parcels in the postwar emergency, inwardly rebels against being the object of eternal charity in a social order that he no longer believes is divinely ordained. Yet it is on this purely individual social service basis that the gigantic postwar refugee problem has been tackled, at least by the international organizations and to a large extent by the nations themselves.

As a full-fledged member of society with some notions of democracy, the European is conscious of having rights. The church appears as ready as ever to show him mercy, but not to champion the basic justice to which he feels entitled. This problem is clearly recognized in many sections of the European church, but one of the greatest deterrents to long-range action is entrenched institutionalism and institutional thinking.

The second reason applies to *the Christian church itself. In*

*most of Europe Christian charity has concentrated so long on the
social evils that it has difficulty focusing its attention on the social good.* We behave as though good exists merely in the struggle
against evil. The attitude of the church toward society is like that
of an indifferent doctor toward a patient who has become so accustomed to being ill that neither the one nor the other can adjust
himself to the idea of a return to health. To be sure, evils must be
squarely faced. But religion that on the social level deals only with
evil is inevitably permeated with all the odors associated with
human failure.

While it is true that Christians have contributed heavily to the
identification and condemnation of a vast array of social evils,
relatively little has been done to identify and promote the highest
social good. By that is meant something that is big enough to
fill the gap in time and space between the redemption of the individual and the coming of the kingdom of God. At only a few
places in Europe, as pointed out in Chapter Two, are Christians
wrestling earnestly to focus their thoughts on this urgent problem
and thus liberate the church from its own spiritual shackles.

The third reason applies to what might be called *the civic responsibility of the church.* As Christian citizens we have learned to
cross-relate the causes and effects of social evils—for example, that
alcohol may produce not only drunkenness but also broken homes,
that gambling may produce not only dishonesty but also dope-
addiction. *What we cannot bring ourselves to confess is that the
roots of these things are to be found in the faulty structure of our
society* and not merely in the weakness of individuals who perhaps
succumb to the temptation of their environment. Our tendency is to
view the present order of things as unalterable because it is divinely
ordained. Somewhere in our religious thinking we evade our Christian responsibility, and our world goes out of control.

Here is our problem again in a slightly different form: Have Christians anything to offer modern society not only as between the redemption of the individual and the coming of the kingdom of God, but also as between the *promise* of the kingdom of God and the *threat* of chaos? William Temple saw the dilemma clearly when, in the midst of the last war, he said, "We tend to follow one or the other of two lines: either we start from a purely ideal conception [of society], and then bleat fatuously about love; or else we start from the world as it is, with the hope of remedying an abuse here or there, and then we have no general direction or criterion of progress."[1] There is a full-grown conviction among Christians in Europe that something must be done through the church for the reordering of society, but as yet it has found no Christian channel of expression.

IS SOCIALISM THE ANSWER?

In Europe the most common name given to the reordering of society is socialism. Indeed, it has become downright venerable. The political parties that bear the name Socialist are, for the most part, so thoroughly domesticated that they are generally regarded as the very essence of reliable respectability. In most countries the Socialists occupy the broad middle-of-the-road that lies between the left radicals (who are usually Communists) and the right radicals (who represent the ultra-conservative interests and the strong leader cults).[2]

In France, for example, the Radical Socialists have not for years been either radical or fearsomely socialistic, but might be described perhaps as progressive republican. By tradition, if you please, the

---

[1] *Christianity and Social Order,* by William Temple, p. 59. London, Student Christian Movement Press, 1950.

[2] These moderate Socialists, incidentally, have been severely persecuted, exiled, tortured, and killed, both by the Nazis and by the Communists.

Socialists are expected to be the first to offer their services to the president whenever the government falls, but there has not been a Socialist premier in France since 1947.

Great Britain had five years of socialization under a Labor regime following World War II, but it is now clear that the Tories will not use their return to power to change much that was done. They draw a careful distinction between the idea of the welfare state and the doctrinaire abstractions of socialism, which are distrusted just as much in Britain as in the United States.

All of prosperous Scandinavia has quietly adhered to a form of benevolent socialism, while retaining the royal families. In Sweden the Socialists are, in theory, committed to complete nationalization of industry and the overthrow of the monarchy; but they would not dream of using their present power to carry their theories into practice. In short, practically all of Europe today is governed or powerfully influenced by political socialism, or, as we shall see later, by political Roman Catholicism, or by a combination of both.

In West Germany the principal opponent of the Christian Democratic Party, which is now in power thanks largely to Allied pressure, is the Social Democratic Party. But here, as elsewhere in Europe, the Socialists have sometimes proved to be more conservative and nationalistic than the so-called reactionary parties.

All of these Western Socialists have unanimously repudiated communism, although they may still regard Karl Marx as their chief prophet. They declare that Russian communism is nothing but state capitalism and therefore—like all capitalism—the enemy of real socialism. In Eastern Europe there can be no doubt that the Socialist parties have all been pressed into Communist-dominated union parties or reduced to quavering insignificance. Consequently, there is a very concrete, practical difference between West European socialism and East European communism. The latter, of course, is still represented in West Europe, chiefly in Italy and France. It must be emphasized that in this chapter we are discussing socialism, *not* Russian communism.

TYPES AND KINDS OF SOCIALISM

There are, as one German essayist points out, at least seven different varieties of socialism. Some of them, like certain types of mushrooms, are considered harmless, but others are poison. In the former category are specimens like Utopian Socialism, which is found only in fictional descriptions of a perfect society, and Conservative Socialism as typified by Bismarck, the Iron Chancellor, whose radicalism might bear some comparison with that of the first Roosevelt. On the poisonous side are the Scientific Socialism of Karl Marx, who foresaw the need of bloody revolutions; then Communism, which is the most virulent form of Marxism. and finally, National Socialism (especially Hitler's), which contained far more nationalism than socialism. The two remaining types are classified as Social Reform, which aims to overhaul the capitalistic system rather than wreck it; and as Christian Socialism, which is an attempt to model social reform after the teachings of Jesus.

It is safe to say that practically the only form of socialism represented in the outstanding socialistic political parties of Western Europe today is Social Reform. Today—after a brief postwar flirtation with communism—West European socialism is very moderate. There are many reasons for this, among which the following are to be found: the dismaying exhibition of totalitarian socialism in Soviet Russia and Nazi Germany; the impressive demonstration of strength and growth in capitalist America, which so far contradicts all Marxian prophecies of doom; and the subtle process by which, in Europe itself, all aging revolutionaries become mild reactionaries, especially under actual governmental responsibility.

What do these Socialists stand for today? Disregarding all official definitions, let me try to describe this modified socialism as it appears in its diluted form to the average European. In this view socialism represents a program of social and economic reform designed to give all men a fair share of the good things of life; moreover, it believes that this can best be accomplished by bringing those industries that are based on natural resources under public ownership and popular control.

At this point, the average American democrat (with a small "d") and the average European socialist (with a small "s") are closer together than they imagine. They certainly agree on the general aims of social control, even though they may differ on the method of executing them. Remember that I am describing the ordinary, humanized, postwar socialism (not scientific Marxism or the theories of dialectical materialism) in an effort to account for the fact that it—rightly or wrongly—is popularly accepted as one of the best answers, if not the only answer, to the political problem of Europe.

Why not call it democracy insteady of socialism? The most direct answer seems to lie in the distinction between two types of liberty— political and economic. Admittedly, the one does not mean much without the other; but, under certain conditions, if a citizen has the one, he may be less concerned about the other. The American mentality, for instance, has been shaped since the 1770's by the supreme desirability of political liberty, largely because Americans have never really felt the heavy chains of economic frustration. Furthermore, the American workman was able to use his political liberty to obtain an increasing measure of economic freedom.

European mentality, on the other hand, has been nourished since the Industrial Revolution on a growing passion for economic liberty. It is less interested in political *responsibility* than in economic *rights*. Influenced today by the teachings of socialism, the European is more inclined to think of his claim on society than of society's claim on him.

At this point we see one of the dangerous flaws in even a modified type of socialism, namely, that it places far more emphasis on rights than on responsibilities. Fortunately, this danger is diminishing today—thanks to the abuses of totalitarianism, which offered economic security in exchange for spiritual slavery. But one of the most discouraging discoveries in connection with the nationalization (public ownership) of coal in Britain was the sharp increase in absenteeism at the mines! The "boss" took the day off whenever he liked, even in the midst of the fuel crisis.

HOW TO INSURE AGAINST INSECURITY

It is exceedingly doubtful whether Britain would ever have come to accept the welfare state so fully, if it had not been for her economic plight. As matters stand now, it is only by contrast to the Bolshevik redness of Russia that Great Britain looks no more than a rosy pink to her American friends. In other words, if it were not for the USSR, the USA, with its capitalist economy, might today regard Great Britain as world enemy number one. On the continent socialism, when it finally got to power, usually turned out to be nothing worse than a left-of-center liberalism. But the Labor Party that held power in Britain from 1945 to 1952 was fully determined to institute a social revolution, and did. "Britain was the first great country where socialism could count on an effective run of power, with a popular mandate, and above all an alert, informed, progressive citizenship whose freedom (read 'democracy') was inviolable." [1] This fact and its consequences merit

---

[1] *Assignment to Austerity*, by Herbert L. Matthews and E. C. Matthews, p. 34. Indianapolis, Bobbs Merrill Co., 1950.

some serious Christian thought in the light of Britain's Christian traditions.

To gain a better appreciation of the attraction of socialism for the British people, let us briefly list a few salient features of their postwar situation. The war was won but at tremendous cost. All foreign investments had been liquidated to pay the war bill, and Britain, which had formerly owned half of all foreign investments in the world, was now a debtor nation to almost the same extent as she had been a creditor nation. Income taxes at war's end took 50 per cent of earnings. (But, owing largely to antiquated methods, the British miner actually took more money in wages out of every ton of coal mined than his American cousin with a far higher standard of living!) The British Isles have a population of 3,000 persons per square mile of *arable* land, but only 7 per cent of its people are engaged in agriculture. Sixty per cent of all food is normally imported, and 80 per cent of all raw material. One-fourth of her shipping was lost in the war, along with most of the empire.

What group of people, faced with even these few facts, would not think seriously about reorganizing their economy so as to derive the maximum benefit from every available asset? Britain was in 1952 the only Western European country where rationing still prevailed, even though it should be added that all other countries have felt the pinch of economic rationing because of spiraling prices that have almost automatically wiped out all wage and salary increases. Rationing in East Europe continues!

Socialist planning represents to Britons and to many other Europeans the only serious and sustained effort to find an answer to two clamorous needs.

The first is for a reasonable degree of personal economic security. You may call it a full life, if you prefer. Periodic unemployment is one of the greatest of all human nightmares. Britain, for example, will never forget the era of the dole during the world depression. In 1942 Archbishop Temple listed three major social evils that the church in Britain could not ignore: namely, bad housing, malnutrition, and unemployment. The third evil he characterized as the "most hideous" of all because, however much a man's physical needs are supplied, the gravest part of the trouble remains: the unemployed feel they are not wanted. "That is the thing that has power to corrupt the soul of any man not already far advanced in saintliness." "In other words," he added, "we are challenged to find a social order which provides employment, *steadily and generally.*" [1] The Labor Party believes that a feeling of social usefulness should be fostered deep into the retirement years and inserted this plank into their election platform in 1946: "The guiding principle of Labor's policy is that old age should not be a burden of loneliness and sorrow, but a period of happiness, rest, and respect after work is done."

The other major longing of Europe's common people is for world peace. Socialism began as an *international* movement to revamp a political and economic order that was based on dog-eat-dog competition. Commercial rivalries were—and are—reputed to be the prime cause of war, whereas socialism aimed to promote the welfare of man by means of cooperative or collective controls. According to the fondest socialist dreams, national states and their boundaries would simply disappear. This, it should be pointed out, has never been true of Labor Party policy in the United Kingdom and it has never been a primary aspect of the socialist program anywhere in Europe, even though hate is today forbidden by law in the "popular democracies" behind the Iron Curtain. Indeed, most socialist parties have become violently national, but it is nevertheless true that one of the outstanding ideals of socialism—

[1] Temple, *op. cit.,* pp. 10-16.

next to its emphasis on economic rights—is its promotion of human fellowship.[1] Is there any hope that it will ever be able to overcome nationalism?

NO SALVATION THROUGH SOCIALISM

How does it stand today with these two ideal goals? It is, to be brief, doubtful whether very many Socialists themselves expect to see the fulfillment of these dreams in the foreseeable future. Quite aside from the handicap of the disastrous effects of two wars—but for which socialism might never have obtained its limited chance —two simple observations appear to condemn it.

In the first place, socialism's welfare state (cradle-to-grave protection) seems to be something that only some degree of free enterprise can pay for. Socialism rarely seems able to create wealth; it usually distributes it.

In the second place, socialism has not succeeded in modifying the East-West crisis. When the showdown came between democracy and totalitarianism, European socialism was split right down its geographical middle. The imperceptible progress of the Benelux negotiations offers no consolation to socialism that even this very limited objective will be reached soon. The Schuman Plan likewise made but slow headway against the determined opposition of the Social Democratic Party in Germany. Perhaps the opponents of socialism in Britain are right who, according to Herbert Matthews, say that it must overcome two fundamental weaknesses: "a lack of technical understanding of the business world, and a failure

---

[1] "The tragedy," according to the report of an Anglican Commission, "is that the fellowship of the Christian church seems to offer them [the people] less in the way of community than is to be found in membership in a political party or trade union. . . . The church lacks the forceful contribution of those who passionately desire community of spirit and the more just ordering of society."—*Christianity Today*, edited by H. S. Leiper, p. 142. New York, Morehouse-Gorham Co., 1947.

to take sufficient account of the tenaciousness of original sin." [1]

In effect, theoretical socialism has failed up till now in fulfilling either the hopes or the fears that had been vested in it. The failure of the hopes is not just a matter of falling short in its self-set goals, and the blame for the failure cannot be laid entirely to outside causes. The reason for failure goes deeper, and failure was inevitable. Why? Because social reform in itself cannot produce a full life nor guarantee security. World peace, moreover, is not merely a matter of making economic plans for the brotherhood of man. In reality, socialism attempted too much; it started off not merely as a reform program but as a plan of secular self-salvation.

SOME CHRISTIAN BEGINNINGS

Various attempts have been made to link socialism to Christianity with considerable benefit to the cause of social justice, but with indifferent political success. In England the contact between Christian faith and social vision had always been close. The history of this contact is well worth tracing from Robert Owen, the nonconformist businessman who left more of a mark on British socialism than his contemporary Karl Marx. He was followed by a remarkable chain of divines led by F. D. Maurice, whose contribution kept socialism in debt to Christian thought, right down to William Temple, whose premature death in 1944 deprived both church and state of an outstanding creative leader. Britain has been singularly fortunate in having among her political and social leaders such representative Christian men as Sir William Beveridge, Sir Stafford Cripps, Lord Halifax, and Mr. Arnold Toynbee—but for all this, there can be no doubt that the church itself has steadily drifted out of the main current of national life.

Heroic efforts have been made to stem this trend, some of which

---

[1] Matthews, *op. cit.,* p. III.

were noted in Chapter Two. One of the most interesting prewar movements was led by Dr. George MacLeod in the Iona Community on the lonely island where St. Columba landed to begin the conversion of Scotland. Iona represents an effort to reunite work and worship in the hearts of men and women who for a few weeks gather together to re-establish a living Christian community and take their newfound sense of fellowship back to the local parishes. England itself produced the Christian Commandos, selected teams that visited particular towns or factories for a brief period in an effort at mass revival and evangelization. The Roman Catholics instituted a similar Sword of the Spirit Movement. The Church of England has its Industrial Christian Fellowship that concentrates on reaching factory employees in the great manufacturing centers, as well as dockers and miners, through a special chaplaincy service. The Church of Scotland alone has put 290 chaplains into industrial plants. These innovations have been widely copied by other European churches.

On the continent, the impact of a Christian contribution to the development of a new social order has been even less perceptible, with the possible exception of Scandinavia. By and large, the rigid doctrinaire lines laid down by Karl Marx and reciprocated in kind by the theologians, have effectively prevented a salutary exchange of views between socialism and Christianity. The Sigtuna Foundation in Sweden represents one of the earliest and best efforts from the church's side to put Christianity back into the center of society. Further mention of Scandinavian socialism will be necessary in the following chapter. In Germany just over a century ago, Johann H. Wichern inspired a most effective form of social service, called the Inner Mission, which developed alongside political socialism and grew into an international movement based principally on a vast network of deaconess mother houses.

At the turn of the century in France there was a remarkable upsurge of social evangelization that found its origins in the collapse of the empire after the Franco-Prussian War in 1871. The McAll Mission pioneered the way toward meeting the laboring man on his own ground by establishing dozens of *salles neutres* (neutral halls) divested of any ecclesiastical trappings. Out of this revival came Le Christianisme Social, which set up *solidarités* and *fraternités* under the leadership of Elie Gounelle in the heart of proletarian neighborhoods—namely, workers' churches. But, with the diminution of outside support, this movement has slowed down. One of the more recent approaches is La Main Tendue, which began in 1935 with the decision of three young women to dedicate themselves to sharing the life of the de-Christianized masses, and which became a recognized adjunct of the Reformed Church in 1949.

TOWARD THE EVANGELIZATION OF SOCIETY

On the whole it was the spiritual descendants of John Calvin— driven by the force of their faith in election by grace—who made the most progress toward the heart of the European problem by experiment with new evangelistic methods. And it was the spiritual descendants of Luther who—with their consciousness of being "miserable sinners"—expounded, extended, and ennobled the high duty of social service toward the individual.

In spite of all such efforts, the sum total of the church's social endeavor in the past century was not adequate to overcome the general impression that the church as such was wary of becoming involved in any serious thinking about a thoroughgoing social renewal. This impression may have been wrong, but it persisted. A few efforts were made in Western Europe to bridge the gulf of suspicion and distrust, but the Socialists up to World War II continued to consider the church a citadel of capitalist reaction and the church continued to regard socialism as a disturber of the peace, if not as a firebrand of anarchic revolution.

It was during the course of these developments that European society ceased to be Christian. While it is true that the moderate Socialists of Europe have recently conceived a reluctant admiration for the church because of its fairly successful resistance to the assaults of fascism during the war, they still think that the place of the church is "in the suburbs." That is, they see the church as an institution that sometimes satisfies the spiritual needs of the people where they reside, but rarely where they work. Occasional visits to factories do not fill this gap, and political collaboration is not enough. Today, for example, in several European countries— such as Belgium, Holland, and Austria, the Socialists and Roman Catholics have joined forces in coalition cabinets. But such political marriages are invariably uncomfortable for both parties and have been relatively barren of truly creative results, except perhaps in Holland.

At this late date there seems to be little reason to think either that old-fashioned Christianity will be socialized or that old-fashioned socialism can be Christianized. Perhaps this is as it should be because of the very nature of the church, but it is doubtful whether the majority of Europeans who traditionally think of themselves as being both Christians and Socialists realize that they are living in a divided house. Their best hope that it will not fall is to be found in the fact that a few Christian pioneers have moved beyond the field of social service and are opening up the unexplored territory between Christian faith and social order in our day.

5

A Re-Vision of State-Church Relations

One of the manifest differences between European and American mentality is the attitude toward history.—Professor Adolf Keller.

If the state is going to become more human, then religion will have to become more divine—Bishop Eivind Berggrav.

MODERN Europe is like a gallery containing specimens of almost every possible state and church relationship, except the one that interests Americans most. France probably comes closest to the American pattern of complete separation, save that in one corner —namely, Alsace and part of Lorraine—the established Lutheran, Reformed, and Roman Catholic Churches still enjoy the full support of the state. These two big provinces did not belong to France at the time of the Disestablishment of Religion in 1905, owing to their annexation by Germany from 1871 to 1918. Since then, sporadic efforts have been made, on the one hand, to carry the separation to its logical conclusion and, on the other hand, to re-establish the church everywhere in France as a public institution with access to public funds. Roman Catholic schools, for example, after obtaining state support during the short-lived Vichy regime, have now succeeded in pressing Parliament into evading the law of separation by granting an annual subsidy to each child of elementary school age.

In Germany, although many charitable institutions derive direct benefits from public funds, the only practical connection between church and state is the collection of church taxes by the state. The nature of the Nazi regime spurred Protestant circles to consider seriously the desirability of cutting even these fiscal strings as soon as the war was over; but it is probably true that with its resources already seriously depleted, the church would have been dealt a crippling blow by an abrupt abolition of the tax system. One very interesting sidelight on the state-church relations in divided Germany today is that the nationwide federation of Lutheran and Reformed churches, known as the Evangelical Church in Germany, still stretches across all the zones and is, in effect, the only national institution that can be said to unite the entire country. Neither in the East nor in the West, fortunately, are the constituent churches of this federation legally subject to the state.

Although no two are alike, every European country exhibits today some form of state-church relationship. This must not be taken to mean that *all churches* receive state support, but rather that *all states* give some form of recognition or support to certain preferred churches. There are many "free" churches in Europe, including Lutheran and Reformed, as well as Methodist, Baptist, and others, which as a matter of principle would not accept funds from the state treasury even if offered. Constituting a small minority of all Protestants, many of their members have to pay regular church taxes while at the same time bearing the full costs of their own independent congregations; but in many cases such "double taxation" can easily be avoided by a simple declaration of membership in a free church. In Germany, for example, even though approximately 90 per cent of the population is to be found in either Roman Catholic, Lutheran, or Reformed churches, there are about 250 other religious bodies, most of them very tiny, that claim freedom of worship. To some of them the existence of church taxes and other forms of public recognition constitute a standing provocation because they have often been most unjustly treated by the so-called state churches.

THE OLD EUROPEAN PATTERN IS ESTABLISHMENT

Strictly speaking, we are at this point discussing the simple facts of church-state relationships, not the question of religious liberty or freedom of the individual conscience. Yet it is entirely relevant to point out that Dr. M. Searle Bates in his magnificent study, *Religious Liberty,*[1] lists the following countries (taking only Western Europe for the moment, excluding overseas colonies) as granting the highest degree of freedom to all faiths: Belgium, Eire, Great Britain, France, Holland, and Switzerland. To these postwar Germany should be added. It is worth noting that this list corresponds very nearly to the bloc of states whose notable similarities made them the basis of the last chapter, and also that they are about equally divided between nominally Catholic and nominally Protestant. Dr. Bates also lists the countries where preferences are recognized but discriminations are not acute: Denmark, Finland, Norway, Sweden, and Yugoslavia. Finally come the countries of acute discrimination: Austria, Greece, and Spain, to which postwar Italy and all the Soviet satellite states should now be added. These listings tend to indicate that there is a direct connection between religious liberty and the relation between state and church.

Returning to the observation that there is not a single country in Europe where complete separation of church and state prevails, let us prepare to focus our attention on the nature and extent of

[1] Published by Harper and Brothers, New York, for the International Missionary Council, 1945.

the state connection and its effect on the church. As the whole question of Roman Catholicism and Eastern Orthodoxy will be raised in subsequent chapters, we can now limit ourselves to the predominantly Protestant lands.

Leaving France and Germany, which have already been mentioned, to one side for the moment, it may be said that England, Scotland, Holland, Switzerland (on a cantonal basis), Denmark, Sweden, Finland, and Norway all have established churches in varying degrees of relationship to the state. In the first-named country the established church is Anglican, in the next three it is Reformed, and in the last four it is Lutheran. In the Netherlands and Switzerland the Roman Catholic Church is established, also, and derives similar benefits from the state.

In the four Scandinavian countries, which are nearly 100 per cent Lutheran,[1] the Protestant state-church relationship comes to clearest expression on a national basis. In each of these countries the population, for one thing, is as homogeneous as in Greece, Spain, or Italy. In fact, Scandinavia provides what is probably the best example of real state-churchism in West Europe, because Lutherans have no church-state pretensions; that is, they are not interested in exercising temporal power. There is a great deal of difference between a state-church mentality and a church-state mentality. Moreover, the Lutheran Church has no Vatican and, consequently, no corresponding drive toward international centralization. No one—the Scandinavians least of all—would seriously

---

[1] *Finland,* which is 96 per cent Lutheran, has 4,000 Methodists, 2,500 Baptists, in addition to 75,000 Orthodox, 1,000 Roman Catholics, and 650 Jews. *Norway,* which counts 3.8 per cent of the population outside the national church, has 25,000 Pentecostals, 20,000 "free" Lutherans, 12,000 Methodists, 8,000 Baptists, 4,905 Roman Catholics, 719 Mormons, 550 Jews, and 23,058 persons completely outside all churches. *Denmark,* which is 97 per cent Lutheran, has small bodies of other Protestants, 25,000 Roman Catholics, and 15,000 outside all churches. *Sweden* has 10,000 Catholics, 11,000 Methodists, 100,000 Swedish Covenants, 100,000 Pentecostals, and 40,000 Baptists.

contend that the offices of the Lutheran World Federation bear any comparison with the Holy See. Except for lively foreign mission and international humanitarian interests, the Lutherans of Scandinavia conceive their first religious duty to be the spiritual care of their own nationals.

This concern of the church for the spiritual welfare of a whole nation and the reciprocal concern of the state for the welfare of the church is the fundamental idea behind the state-church relationship in Europe, and is firmly supported by tradition. The Archbishop of York, for instance, summarizes the chief reasons for establishment under two main headings: first, that the state "has responsibility for the spiritual and moral welfare of its people, but as it cannot discharge this duty by itself, it should therefore hand it over to a church"; and second, the state needs a church that "has the right both to exhort and warn it to follow in the ways of righteousness, truth, and mercy." Then he lists certain qualifications that an established church should possess in order to fulfill its task properly: namely, antiquity, catholicity, a widespread parish system covering the country, and the adherence of a majority of the population.[1] These factors possess a validity in Europe that they do not possess in the United States, and the fact that earnest and active Christians hold to them must be respected. Before centering our attention on the state-church situation today, a few remarks about the past appear to be in order.

FROM CONSTANTINE TO QUISLING

The original link between church and state in Europe was forged by Emperor Constantine, who in A.D. 313 issued the Edict of Milan making Christianity legal and, in effect, the religion of

---

[1] *Church and State in England,* by Cyril Garbett, pp. 24-25. London, Hodder and Stoughton, Ltd., 1950.

the Roman Empire. For a few centuries thereafter the empire effectually ruled the Christian church. Then some outstandingly able popes in their struggle for ecclesiastical independence paved the way to a complete reversal of this relationship. For a few centuries thereafter the church ruled the empire, until the gradual crystallization of independent nation states successfully challenged the political power of the papacy and contributed to the Protestant Reformation.

It does not follow that the concept of complete separation between church and state is necessarily a Protestant principle: it is an American principle. The Reformation was a revolt against the church itself, not against the state. But it resulted in the first attempt to distinguish between the duties of the national state and those of an evangelical church. It also defined the relation of a Christian citizen toward civil authorities. Thus, the democratic idea developed.

Limitations of time and space prohibit a discussion of the basic Protestant doctrines regarding church and state. It is frequently supposed that Lutheran doctrine teaches perpetual submission to the state (as a divine order given to us because we are imperfect) and that the Reformed ideal requires that the state (as a divine order, which therefore must be perfect) defer to the church as the symbol of God's sovereignty. Neither of these oversimplified assumptions does full justice to the spirit of the great Reformers, and both of them can be belied by modern example. To be sure, there were times when churches and states confused their respective functions, but fortunately the basic principle of evangelical liberty gradually gained ground and today is in a position to challenge—directly or indirectly—the worst evils of totalitarianism, no matter whether it takes the form of absolute dictatorship or theocratic experiment.

That the church bears a special responsibility toward the state has always been obvious, but it remains a moot question as to whether the church can best exercise this responsibility through a special attachment to the state. Here is the central question of this chapter. As long as governments preserved a friendly attitude toward the church and did not intervene in internal matters, the majority of European churchmen held to the belief that the advantages of a state connection outweighed the disadvantages.

Recent history, however, has amply demonstrated that the nature of the state has been changing and that unsuspected pitfalls await not only the loyal state church today, but even the state-church mentality. Adolf Hitler, who talked glibly about "positive Christianity," had this mentality. He assumed that the church should automatically reflect the policies of the state. Vidkun Quisling picked up the idea and tried to apply it in Norway. Whereas plenty of people, including clergy, agreed with the German Führer, practically none followed his Norwegian puppet. There were various reasons for this, but one of them went back to the fact that a group of Lutheran and Reformed pastors had assembled at Barmen in Germany in the early days of the Nazi regime to re-examine the relationship between church and state. The six-point declaration that they composed there marks another important stage in the struggle for religious liberty. Since the end of the war in both Norway and Germany, as well as throughout Europe, the struggle for full Christian liberty goes on, but scepticism as to the wisdom of complete separation is actually increasing. What does this portend?

Two very practical problems having to do with total separation go a long way to explain the hesitation in Germany at least, and are certainly as weighty as history itself: namely, the financial and educational consequences of total disestablishment. They will be discussed a little later. Meanwhile, it must not be lightly assumed —and this applies to Scandinavia—that a clean-cut division between church and state constitutes an automatic guarantee of a strong revival of pure Christianity. Such revivals have not occurred in France or Germany where the state-church ties are very slender, nor even among the free churches in Britain and on the continent. Following the first world war the free churches in Europe experienced a powerful evangelistic impulse, but the few years since World War II have served to demonstrate that these bodies, except for some of the newer gospel movements, are subject to the same spiritual ailment as the so-called state churches: namely, a complete inability to reach people outside the framework of Christendom. As indicated in Chapter Two, the day of old-fashioned revival is passed, no matter who tries it.

On the other hand, the Europeans who of their own accord are returning to the Christian faith are searching for spiritual security rather than spiritual adventure, and consequently they seem to prefer the older, traditional churches rather than the smaller, newer bodies. If this movement within the church can be interpreted as a part of the trend toward a greater unity in Europe—and I think it can be so interpreted—it seems obvious that the silken shackles of Constantine may perhaps continue to link the church to the state, at least in Western Europe, for many years to come. This fateful development would then give new relevance to the implications contained in the arguments advanced by the Archbishop of York, and serious thought should be given to the question: *Does* the state bear responsibility for the spiritual welfare of its people, and *should* it help to maintain the voice that warns and admonishes it? Can it be possible that the answer is Yes in Europe and No in America? Let's look at the facts and try to let them speak for themselves.

THE GARDEN OF SWEDEN

In Scandinavia the issue emerges rather clearly, because the imperative reasons for retaining the state-church relation are neither financial nor educational, important as both of these reasons may be. In no other area of Europe has the religious development of a whole nation been so tranquil. When the Reformation movement reached Sweden, for example, the entire church embraced it without serious opposition, and the transition to Protestantism was so smooth that the line of apostolic succession remained unbroken. Today the Lutheran Archbishopric of Uppsala—like the Anglican Archbishopric of Canterbury—is generally recognized as one of the most distinguished and historic offices in the Christian church.

While the Protestant church does not agree with the Roman Catholic doctrine that tradition has equal value with the Gospels, traditions of this sort cannot simply be disregarded. In fact, they should be cherished. It is a remarkable fact that the structure of the Church of Sweden, as it is officially called, has never been violently disrupted either by accident or design, and it is in the light of this fact that the anachronistic connection between church and state must be viewed.

The church is defined in Sweden as the state performing its religious functions. The definition is reversible: the state in the performance of its religious functions is the church. A medieval glory pervades the thought—which is shared by the Anglican Church—that the church is the visible expression of God's care for a whole nation and that the church has an obligation to all the people whether they recognize it or not. But unhappily the concept in its modern setting seems utterly bereft of the popular support that an effective state-church should have, except perhaps in some of Sweden's rural areas.

From any free-church viewpoint, the modern Swedish pastor is the paid servant of the state who, in addition to preaching from a prescribed text to an appalling number of empty pews on the average Sunday, is expected to keep the parish records meticulously because the government has no other office of vital statistics. He has the privilege of instructing the entire younger generation in religion, but most of them disappear from sight after confirmation. And he is expected to conduct funeral services for the 99 per cent of the population who take a Christian burial for granted. In Stockholm it has sometimes happened that a pastor has had ten funeral services on a single Sunday.

These are but a few of the least enviable aspects of ecclesiastical establishment that the heavy hand of history imposes on this kind of church.

Another phenomenon in Sweden—almost incredible and one against which a living faith must struggle—is the general prosperity prevailing among the people. What relation, if any, does it bear to the religious development of the country? No one begrudges a people prosperity, but in this case it was political socialism that over a period of twenty years effectively achieved in the northern states what it merely has promised to produce in other parts of Europe: namely, a good social order. The more hard-bitten Scandinavian socialists would say that this was done in spite of, rather than with the help of, the state church.

Sweden, of course, has had no real taste of twentieth century war, thus differentiating her from her three closest neighbors. Although her economy has been adversely affected by international inflation and an influx of refugees, the Queen of the North is today the rosy picture of national good health and cosy comfort. Rich by Scandinavian standards, her wealth is evenly distributed. Generally speaking, her people are prosperous; socially speaking, they are fully protected; politically speaking, they are technically neutral; and religiously speaking, they are complacently tolerant. What more could socialism desire? A marvelous system of cooperatives has grown up; poverty and slums are practically non-existent; an extremely effective social insurance plan is in operation for all. In addition to all this, the people with very few exceptions still belong to one church that is in the advantageous position— according to some defenders of the system—of being officially recognized. Such a combination of religious unity, economic well-being, and political tranquillity is rare among the nations of Europe. In fact, one would think that Sweden has nothing left to wish for on this earth.

Yet, upon closer examination, the situation is, in its basic aspects, not essentially different from that of the countries that bore the brunt of World War II. The only difference is that neutral Sweden seems to be one step further removed from ugly realities and to that extent the people are living in a false paradise. For one thing, good political order at home is no longer a reasonable guarantee of international security. It is not necessary to describe Sweden's unenviable new position as Russia's neighbor—the annoying barrier still blocking the Kremlin's way to the North Atlantic and an industrious beehive full of honey almost irresistably toothsome to a hungry bear. Suffice to say that the Communist vote has dropped from 11 per cent in 1946 to 4.8 per cent in 1951, much faster than in Italy or France.

Sweden's first postwar efforts to cultivate friendly relations with the USSR cooled off rapidly as various other borderline states "went East." Nevertheless, the state is clinging desperately to its neutrality, even to the extent of refusing to join in the United Nations resolutions denouncing Red China as an aggressor in the Korean War. At least the Swedes belong to the UN, whereas the

Swiss do not. On the whole, it can be said that Scandinavia's sympathies—including Sweden's—are with the West and that communism today constitutes a very small internal danger on the territory of the established Protestant churches.[1] The disappearance of two Swedish planes over the Baltic Sea in June, 1952, alarmed the entire country. What danger there is, at the present time, is wholly external, despite sensational espionage trials. This much can be said without raising the question as to how much credit for arresting the spread of a purely Marxist faith goes to the established church and how much to successful state socialism.

ILL AT EASE IN ZION

Nevertheless, when all this has been taken into account, the visitor to Sweden retains a lingering impression of what, for lack of a better term, might be called spiritual uncertainty and unrest, the source of which is definitely internal rather than external. Spiritual uncertainty—using the word spiritual in its widest sense—is common enough in Europe and the Americas also, but in Sweden it seems rather incongruous, at least to the outside observer, in the light of the factors already noted: namely, religious harmony, economic prosperity, and internal security. In a certain sense, Sweden is too well off.

One is tempted to imagine that if Europe could be transformed into a large and sunny Sweden all problems would simply disappear. But the perennial unrest of man is not so easily stilled. In Sweden this fact is reflected in the usual social symptoms: a

---

[1] It is an interesting footnote to church history that the Swedish Communists in Parliament in 1951 opposed an increase in pastors' salaries, whereas the Communists in the Danish Parliament about the same time took the view that, as long as they had a state church, *all* state officials should be decently paid. Meanwhile in Lutheran Iceland the Communist Party—third largest—was savagely attacking the whole church.

substantial index of alcoholism, a rising divorce rate (but not yet to be compared with that in the United States), a surprisingly high percentage of illegitimate births, and a postwar increase in juvenile delinquency. How can these social aberrations, especially an increase of them, be reconciled with such a combination of Christian doctrine and socialist practice, unless it is clearly acknowledged that—at bottom—the spiritual requirements of man can never fully be met by governmental provision for his welfare?

There is the illustrative example of a few devoutly Christian women who volunteered for refugee service in bomb-battered Germany, saying that there was nothing more for them to do at home! The government took care of everything. State socialism, they added, is "social service without love." As a matter of fact, hundreds of Swedish Christian workers are still engaged in various forms of loving social service alongside public welfare agencies, and they are still needed, but a feeling of redundancy is at times inescapable. Perhaps it is caused by the conviction that the social state will sooner or later try to take them over entirely.

Therefore, the question that is occupying many thoughtful Swedish Christians is: what is the proper place of a church, especially a state church, in a situation like this? Hostile Socialists—including outstanding professors in state universities, government officials, and leading editors—seem to entertain no doubts regarding the function of the church: namely, as a sort of fifth wheel on the wagon of society.

In 1951, the Swedish bishops released a special statement on family life and proceeded to deal with the associated problems of divorce, adultery, artificial insemination, and other social problems. It was the first such pastoral letter issued by Swedish church leaders in recent times, and it aroused a storm of protest in secular quarters. Not so much because of some of the ideas contained in the statement, but because the bishops had dared to publish such a letter at all! It is not hard to predict that if these voices were to prevail in a supposedly Christian Sweden, the result would be total victory for the state and total defeat for the church. The church would, in effect, have nothing to do but pray.

For years the Church of Sweden has had to contend with a notoriously hostile Socialist press. One Christian periodical, in trying to analyze this spirit of animosity, expresses the opinion that it is not so much a matter of deep personal conviction with the present generation of younger newspapermen as an acquired journalistic tradition! This anti-church sentiment exists elsewhere in the northern states also, but it is no more vociferous anywhere than it is in Sweden, where the church is most closely tied to the state.

All other Protestant establishments in Europe enjoy relative freedom compared with the Church of Sweden. It is true that the Anglican Church is not able to change the Prayer Book without the consent of Parliament—which was refused in 1926!—and that pastors in various cantons of Switzerland are sworn both to preach the pure gospel and to fulfill their office in the provincial church for the welfare of the Vaterland; [1] but the Swedish Church Assembly cannot meet unless convened by the government and then has the legal right only to veto or accept the laws already dealt with by Parliament.

If Sweden has been singled out, perhaps somewhat unfairly, as an extreme example of state-churchism, it is no exaggeration to say that the state-church mentality, which prevails there, persists throughout Europe and has unquestionably sapped the vitality of

[1] A considerable argument in the Canton of Berne in 1951 revolved around the right of certain churchmen (followers of Karl Barth), who receive their salaries from public funds, to express opinions that might be injurious to Swiss neutrality and the country's democratic form of government.

the Christian witness. That, however, is not the last word to be said on this subject.

THE TIE THAT BINDS

The complete separation of church and state is not an immediate prospect anywhere in Scandinavia, but this does not imply that the Christians of Northern Europe are indifferent toward either the danger or the injustices inherent in the situation. The active free churches, which have frequently had to labor under onerous sanctions, have continually pressed for full religious liberty. Their numbers are not large but their very presence has been salutary. Representative Scandinavian state-churchmen, for their part, have not only waged a valiant struggle for many years against gargantuan city parishes including up to 100,000 ostensible members,[1] but they have been extremely uneasy about their technical monopoly in religious matters.

Considerable progress has already been made in the direction of greater freedom both for the state church itself and for those who are not interested in being part of it.

Finland is farthest along. The Lutheran Church, declared a state church in 1686, obtained considerable freedom as early as 1869. Today the church conducts its own affairs and only with great regret decided recently to petition the state to collect the church tax (one per cent of wages or salary!) along with other taxes. It found that only 60 per cent of its budget was covered following the surrender of much church property for the resettlement of refugees. Bishops, however, are still appointed by the president of the republic from a panel of nominations presented to him by the

---

[1] Not long ago a venerable Danish pastor recalled on the sixtieth anniversary of his ordination that he once served a parish of 80,000 souls in Copenhagen and had not only to conduct regular services on Sunday, but had as many as 40 baptisms, 10 marriages, and 15 funerals in one day!

church, and the national Parliament approves or disapproves church laws submitted to it. This is state control at its lightest.

The Danish church, according to its constitution of 1849, still stands under partial state control but has become increasingly democratic through the foundation of local parish councils and calls itself a peoples' church. This means that all persons are considered as members of the Lutheran Church unless they expressly declare their adherence to some other religious body. Ecclesiastical affairs are in the hands of a state official, and Parliament lays down the church laws. The minister for church affairs appoints pastors from nominations presented to him by the vacant parishes and all salaries are fixed by the state. Income is derived from three sources: church taxes paid by all members, revenue from church property, and the remaining 15 per cent from the state treasury. When new buildings must be erected, the state sometimes pays half the cost, but most of the churches in the capital city have been financed through free-will offerings. After an eight-year ban on church construction because of postwar building restrictions, five new churches are being planned for suburban Copenhagen alone. When the big parishes are cut in half, it has been found that attendance increases by as much as 50 per cent.

In Norway, Parliament votes the church budget but has no jurisdiction over internal affairs. Nominally the king governs the church, authorizes the order of worship and the hymnal, and appoints pastors on the advice of the bishops after consultation with the congregation concerned. The term national church is used to describe this relationship. Norwegians have been free to leave the church since 1845, and Roman Catholics, whose numbers have quadrupled in the past fifteen years, have had the privilege of public worship since 1843, although Jesuits are still barred by law. Certain church reforms, designed to set up responsible diocesan and national offices, are now being carefully studied. These executive offices would replace the advisory councils established in 1933 and thus place much more control in the hands of the church itself. Heretofore, neither in Norway nor Denmark could the state church be said to have had a responsible ecclesiastical head!

THE QUEST FOR GREATER FREEDOM

Thus the trend of affairs in Scandinavia is definitely in the direction of less state interference and more freedom. For the sake of all concerned, the leadership within the church has gladly consented and collaborated in the relaxation of outdated and galling restrictions.

A noteworthy step forward was taken in Sweden when, on January 1, 1952, a new law went into effect whereby each Swedish citizen obtains full privilege "freely to exercise his religion," and, if he so desires, to abstain from all religious association. Since 1726 state-church membership had been prescribed for all citizens, although rights were granted to certain minority bodies in 1860. Now for the first time a Swede can resign from the state church without declaring his intention to join some other religious fellowship.[1] He would then pay only 40 per cent of the state-church tax as a charge against normal civil registration, which remains a parish responsibility. Teachers in public schools need no longer be members of the state church, and government officials up to ministerial rank can likewise be chosen from the non-Lutherans, except for the minister of religion and education. All children of state-church members are considered to be church members until the age of fifteen, but may then resign. Ordained ministers of

[1] The free church bodies of Sweden promptly voted to enjoin their adherents to resign officially from the state church in order to clarify their status, but no rapid exodus has occurred.

all faiths may perform marriages that are valid in civil law, and the Roman Catholics may found monasteries and convents (banned since 1595). In October, 1951, for the first time broadcasting of the Roman Catholic service over the state radio took place.

No less noteworthy is the tone taken by Archbishop Brilioth in the course of a radio broadcast shortly after the new law took effect. "It is evident," he said, "that the religious situation in our country today is different from that which prevailed when the church law of Charles XI made it a duty for every Swede to belong to the church. The principle of religious liberty is precious to us. The church can gain nothing in retaining by force of law those who reject her message. . . . The church does not wish to precipitate a change in the age-old association with the state, but it should stand out even more clearly than before as being the church . . . and not merely a state institution for religious care."

But perhaps the most convincing proof that the Scandinavians are in dead earnest as regards justice and liberty was delivered during the war. When Fascism invaded Scandinavia in the spring of 1940, Christian resistance was not long in letting its influence be felt. The story of Danish and Norwegian opposition to the Nazi conquest is too fresh in memory to require repetition.

The outstanding symbol of opposition in each country was a clergyman: Pastor Kaj Munk and Bishop Eivind Berggrav. Who can forget how at Easter in 1942 all but 64 of the 861 Norwegian ministers unhesitatingly laid down their state offices and their state salaries, declaring at the same time that they would continue to be pastors to their people? Or how Bishop Berggrav, standing before Vidkun Quisling, calmly replied, "Here I am!" when the little Hitler in helpless anger shouted, "You triple traitor! You deserve to have your head chopped off!"

Who can forget the peculiar parson of a tiny village in Jutland —Denmark's foremost playwright—who, when he received a circular letter from the Minister for Church Affairs advising all Danish pastors to maintain a neutral attitude with regard to Quisling's attacks on the Norwegian church, responded that he had absolutely no intention of complying? He added, "If for fear of men I should remain a passive spectator, I would feel myself unfaithful and blameworthy, that is to say, a criminal toward my Christian faith, my Danish soul, and my pastor's vow." And who can forget how Kaj Munk was finally arrested, interrogated, put into a car at night, shot to death, and his body thrown into a ditch?

THE FINANCIAL AND EDUCATIONAL CONSEQUENCES

The lessons learned during the war years have not been forgotten either by the state or by the church. In the midst of economic rehabilitation, Scandinavia has been quietly and slowly reappraising her institutions and her spiritual as well as her physical resources. Superficially, the job of postwar reconstruction was accomplished with amazing speed. Despite the fact that Finland suffered enormously in its two wars with the USSR, and both Norway and Denmark were invaded and occupied for four to five years by the Nazis, these three countries on their own initiative have regained their financial footing and are getting along remarkably well.[1]

Finland especially has done an astounding job with a minimum of international attention. Having lost 14 per cent of her territory, she took in 480,000 refugees—more than any other country except

[1] If the four northern states would unite, they would be the largest country in Europe, with an area greater than France but a population only one-third as large. Natural resources are not very rich. Although Denmark is fairly fertile, less than 3 per cent of Norway's land is arable and only 9 per cent of Sweden's. See *The State of Europe*, by Howard K. Smith, pp. 176-183. London, Cresset Press, Ltd., 1950.

Germany. Without recourse to any international refugee organization or other agency, she has already given them new land up to four-fifths of what they had lost, to say nothing of making gigantic reparations payments to Russia, now completed.

In the light of the Finnish church's appeal to the state to help collect the church taxes in order to balance the ecclesiastical budget, we can more easily appreciate the situation in other areas of Europe where churches are battling impoverishment and a rising cost of living. Some knowledge of the salary standards of pastors in countries like France and Austria (about $60 per month) will lead inevitably to the conclusion that financial relief is urgent. This makes more comprehensible the reluctance in many quarters of the German church to surrender a measure of financial security if, at the same time, the danger of state control can be avoided.

In recent years the Lutherans in Austria and even the Reformed in well-to-do Switzerland have sought the help of the state in establishing a church tax to cope with the vexing problem of ecclesiastical finances in the midst of a galloping inflation. The likelihood of raising adequate funds among church members on a voluntary basis seems, at the present time, utterly unrealistic, although many church leaders appear to be convinced that this will someday be necessary and that a determined start should be made now.

The story of the gradual development of church offerings into church taxes makes interesting reading and has a simple logic of its own. Assuming that the whole population of a given area belongs to one church—as is frequently true even today in large parts of Europe[1]—why should not the common church be supported by a common levy? There is an element of genuine socialism

---

[1] The mammoth movements of refugees after World War II have played a tremendous role in scrambling the confessions of Europe.

in this. Certainly, general taxation is infinitely preferable to the medieval system of patronage by noble families! The tax was, and is, so low that many Europeans would rather pay it than put themselves to the slight inconvenience of arranging not to do so.

The Europeans—including the most active church members (always excepting the free-church minority)—are simply not trained to the idea of supporting their churches themselves, except through taxes, and they instinctively think of the services of the church as something that comes to them free of cost through the state. Many European churchmen would like to inaugurate the idea of a church based on the voluntary offerings of its members, but in the midst of postwar poverty it is hard to propose it.

It must frankly be confessed that without state support—if only in the form of tax collections—the European church could not possibly have emerged from its recent crisis as well as it has. Financially, it owes far more to the state than it does to gifts from abroad. Here again history and tradition have played a fateful role. Europe is still full—despite bombings—of magnificent and not-so-magnificent, but equally expensive, ancient church edifices.

Thus, the hard fact is, regardless of all debate about the relative merits of offerings and taxes, that the average established church trembles at the thought of entrusting itself to the undeveloped sense of stewardship of its indifferent masses. In general, they are willing to pay—at most—the equivalent of a few dollars per year in taxes, but in relatively few instances would they appear in church to place even that much on the collection plate.[1] While the church was training its members to bring gifts, there would be almost a complete lack of funds to meet costs of operation.

Aside from financial assistance, the most important single advantage that accrues from a state and church connection is coop-

[1] See Chapter 1, p. 7.

eration in the field of education. In no country—least of all in the United States—has this problem been satisfactorily solved. Christians everywhere agree that the best Christian education should be made available to all children, but how? One of the answers, of course, is to support church schools from public funds. Europe has tried every conceivable solution to this apparently insoluble problem. Holland fought for eighty years to assimilate the church schools and ended by subsidizing them. But new and fairly satisfactory solutions have been put into effect in both Great Britain and Sweden recently.

In the latter country there are compulsory daily devotions, from which pupils can be withdrawn at the request of parents, and also two hours of instruction each week in the "whole content" of Christian knowledge, presenting it as an evangelical message but without particular confessional characteristics. Thus the liberal moralizing that during the past thirty years took the place of old-fashioned dogmatic Lutheranism will, in its turn, be replaced by something more positive.

Much the same trend of thought is apparent in the British Education Act passed in 1944, whereby a daily worship service is provided in all primary and secondary schools, and a course of religious instruction is to be worked out by the school authorities and local churches. The established churches rightly fear that a complete separation from the state would probably bring a drastic change in their ability to provide at least a minimum of religious training for a majority of the nation's children.

SURVEYING THE NEW BOUNDARIES

If, for a variety of reasons, there seems to be little likelihood of complete separation of church and state anywhere in Europe, is there good ground for hoping that the church is better prepared to resist encroachments by the state? The answer in England is, characteristically, a cautious warning against precipitate action that may do the church itself more harm than good. The Assembly of the Church of England, after studying the state-church situation, summed up its findings by saying that establishment has conspicuous merits and conspicuous dangers, but that, on balance, the merits outweigh the dangers. The free churches of Britain read the report, too, and asked themselves whether they should again take the initiative in demanding the disestablishment of the Church of England. The Secretary of the Baptist Union, Dr. Ernest Payne, laid down three reasons why this seemed inadvisable: (1) We are in a dangerous transitional period in regard to the theory and activity of the state; (2) The churches are not of one mind on the nature of the church, but nevertheless are endeavoring to reach agreement in the framework of inter-church councils; (3) A religious controversy, involving the status and powers of the Crown, would be disastrous at the beginning of a new reign.[1]

The churches of Britain live not only by faith, but by confidence in the state. On the continent this same degree of trust no longer pertains, thanks to the closer experience of fascism and communism. Consequently, the church shows signs of bracing itself more firmly against the state and its encroachments into the realm that belongs to religion.

Two of Europe's outstanding churchmen, who bear the scars of totalitarianism on their bodies, have laid down their war-born convictions in thought-provoking studies of the modern state. Both of them think that the modern state has run amok and that the church must help to fix the frontiers beyond which it has no right to venture.

[1] From an address before the Assembly of the Congregational Union of England and Wales, May, 1952.

Bishop Dibelius, who stands in the midst of the East-West tur-moil in the divided city of Berlin, has staked out these boundaries very plainly.[1] He notes the drift toward totalitarianism, of which all European churchmen are acutely aware, and he relentlessly divests the modern state of the myths that conceal its true nature. The state, he points out, is nothing more than the machinery of civil government, which must be kept under strict control by the people it is to serve, not dominate. After ridiculing the notion that the state in itself is the stout champion of justice, of morality, of the arts and sciences, Bishop Dibelius mentions five limits at which the state must stop: it must stop at the church door in matters of religious liberty; it must stop at the family threshold in matters of education for life (although state funds must provide for the schools, teachers, and educational facilities); it must stop at the judge's bench, where justice can be pronounced only in God's name, not in the name of the state; it must stop at the factory gate when-ever it ceases to protect legitimate enterprise and begins to control all commerce and industry by force; and it must stop short at the very thought of making charity its own monopoly.

Can there ever be a really good, effective relationship between church and state? Bishop Berggrav proposes an extension of the federal principle in both church and state.[2] The renewed church in Norway, he says, is being re-established not on the nation but on the Bible and on 10,000 local Christian societies. It is being built from the bottom up, not from the top down. The church itself is thus federated, not monolithic or autocratic, and therefore a good example to the state. Maybe that is the biggest contribution the church can make to the modern state: a good example of Chris-tian democracy anchored in the life of the local congregation.

[1] *Die Grenzen des Staates,* by Otto Dibelius. Furche Verlag, 1949.
[2] *Man and State,* by Eivind Berggrav. Philadelphia, Muhlenberg Press, 1950.

6

Where Error Has No Rights

In Catholicism we see the tradition of Rome, and in the authority of the Vatican the only universal idea in the world.—Benito Mussolini.

Protestants are caught between black and red reaction.—An Italian Protestant.

PROTESTANTS show an amazing tendency to sink from sight in Latin Europe. This applies not only to the indigenous Protestants but, strangely enough, to the visitors also. Thousands of Protestant tourists crossed the Alps into Italy during the Holy Year, taking understandable advantage of the special travel rates, and were counted as pilgrims. I went to Rome that spring and discovered that all six "pilgrims" in my compartment were Swiss Reformed.

The same remarkable transformation affected postwar relief supplies from America. Upon arrival in Italy, even the food and clothing donated by United States Protestants and conveyed in UNRRA or International Red Cross trucks were frequently rebaptized as "Gifts from the Holy Father." Not even the fact that the shipments originated in America became generally known in certain areas where overzealous Roman Catholics had charge of the distribution.

Admittedly, the number of Protestants in Latin Europe is exceedingly slim. There are only about 1,600,000 in all of Portugal, Spain,

France, Belgium, Italy, and the French cantons of Switzerland, among a combined population of 128 million people. In fact, if you subtract France and Switzerland, the total number of Protestants in the remaining four countries, including Spain and Italy, drops to about 114,000 (certainly not more than 162,000) in an ocean of 86 million Catholics.[1] Multiply the latter figure by two and you obtain approximately the present United States population; multiply the former figure by two and you can imagine how much of an impact 220,000 Protestants would be able to make on the whole of the United States if it were solidly Roman Catholic. Nevertheless, the Protestants in Latin Europe have exercised an influence far out of proportion to their size, and the total number of sympathizers is far greater than the professed members.

The numbers are small enough, but that is not the only reason why Protestants display an alarming tendency to disappear. In 1901 there were 65,595 Evangelicals registered in Italy; in 1911, owing largely to strong outside missionary activity, the number rose to 123,253; but by 1931 it dropped back to 82,569! An even more remarkable phenomenon is recorded in this official census: in 1901 there were 830,000 registered as atheists or indifferent to religion; in 1911 more than one and one-half million declared themselves without religion; but in 1931 this whole category dropped to only 17,483! Evidently a tremendous return to Rome had occurred, but a scrutiny of modern church history does not reveal any record of it. What really happened was that a change was made in the census tabulation. After having been omitted altogether in 1920, the religious question was reinserted in 1931 in the form of a simple inquiry about baptism. Even Protestant pastors were thereupon regis-

---

[1] Belgium 27,000 Protestants, perhaps more; France about 1,000,000; Italy 60,000 to 100,000; Portugal 7,000 to 15,000; Spain at least 20,000; Switzerland (in French cantons) 500,000.

tered as Roman Catholics if they had been so baptized in infancy.[1] Despite the protests of Protestants, this form was used again in 1951! One of the Italian newspapers published the following paragraph under the heading, "Liberty of Parish."

Thereby the inscription of the whole Italian population in the registers of the Catholic Church becomes an accomplished fact. They were not asked which was their religion, nor whether they had any, because from the outset it is assumed that an Italian citizen could not be anything but Roman, Catholic, Apostolic. . . . The religious denomination, actually, is rapidly passing from the state of personal attribute to one of general nomenclature. . . . In this way, the responsibility of the parish will soon become identical with the responsibilities of the civilian registration office, and people will not be considered as really "born" and "citizens" if they are not able to prove that they are also "baptized" and "members" in a parish.[2]

By similar tactics, Spain used to recognize the existence of only 2,000, instead of 20,000 Protestants. For the first time, in 1952, the existence of 20,000 was officially admitted, although an attempt was made to minimize the importance of the figure by saying that half of them are foreigners, which is far from being the case.

We have noted that Methodists, for example, have been registered as Lutherans in Sweden until very recently. This and other similarities between northern and southern Europe are taken to indicate that Protestants should move out of their glass houses before they begin to throw bricks. Perhaps so, but too hasty conclusions should be avoided pending further examination of differences that far outweigh these similarities. For this purpose, the present status of Protestantism in Latin Europe should be described briefly, as well as its relationship to Roman Catholicism.

---

[1] *Christianity Today*, edited by Henry S. Leiper, pp. 75-76. New York, Morehouse-Gorham Co., 1947.
[2] *Il Mondo*, November 24, 1951.

LATIN EUROPE BETWEEN FREEDOM AND FRANCO

First, a very few words about the Swiss. Although there is a Latin Switzerland, not only is the entire country predominantly Protestant, but even the French-speaking cantons have a Reformed majority (500,000 out of 930,000), and freedom is about as complete as it is humanly possible to obtain.

In two of the remaining five Catholic states—namely Belgium and France, to which Luxembourg might be added—the Protestant churches are entirely free of oppressive strictures and actually receive financial support. Such freedom has existed for more than 100 years in Belgium, but the Protestant community is still tiny and very much split into independent churches, only the largest of which receives state subsidies for the upkeep of its buildings and the salaries of its 22 pastors. A hundred years ago there were only four parishes.

Since 1925 evangelical instruction has been permitted in the public schools, and today 54 pastors or evangelists, who are reimbursed by the state, are recognized as teachers of religion in more than 100 schools. As noted before, the Republic of France has had a law of separation since 1905 when all Protestant pastors, like the Roman priests, lost their state salaries, except in Alsace-Lorraine. State officials usually show themselves equally ready to hear the Protestant or Catholic side of any question. In both Belgium and France the clergy sometimes cultivate interchurch contacts that can be classified as above and beyond the call of courtesy. In France on a number of occasions joint declarations have been made to the government by Catholics and Protestants.

The Republic of Portugal for a long time was a strange mixture of official Roman Catholicism and anti-clerical officialdom. Catholic influence seems to be increasing again, if the law of July, 1951, whereby all Protestant permits to build must be granted by the minister of the interior, is any indication. The small Protestant communities are given the silent treatment and pursue their course as unobtrusively as possible. The number of Portuguese who attend services without daring to become publicly attached to the evangelical congregations is surprisingly large.

Yet it is a significant fact that in all three of these "liberal" countries where—for shorter or longer periods of time—the evangelical faith has been free to develop, no tremendous inroads have been made upon the nominally Catholic population. Viewing this obvious fact solely from the standpoint of general expediency, ordinary tolerance, and good public relations, one wonders why the Roman Church is at such pains to oppose the Protestants in Italy and Spain. But there are other reasons, as we shall see.

Italy and Spain are undoubtedly the strongholds of Latin Catholicism in Europe. Despite their modern constitutions, which pay lip service to freedom of religion, the governments and their recognized churches have actively concerted together to penalize and suppress any defection from the True Faith. Here it is not merely a matter of antiquated laws and general inertia, but of up-to-date policy. Prewar religious restrictions based on Mussolini's 1920 bargain with the Vatican are still in force in Italy. This concordat with Fascism restored to Roman Catholicism the privileges and prerogatives it had lost sixty years earlier, and revoked the freedom that the Protestants had won in 1870.

In December, 1951, the President of the Baptist World Alliance went to the Italian Minister of the Interior, Signor Scelba, to describe the difficulty of obtaining building permits for placing chapels in certain localities. Signor Scelba then assured him not only of his intention to carry out the provision of the new constitution concerning religious liberty, but offered the services of his ministry to investigate any local difficulties. Such help is badly needed, as the trouble is more in the church's attitude than in that of the state.

State radio monopoly offers another touchstone of religious freedom even more ticklish than building permits. Immediately after the war, at the instance of Allied military authority, Protestant bodies—including the Pentecostals—were given access for the first time to the radio broadcasting stations in Italy. In the last few years their difficulties have multiplied. Hours of service were subject to change without notice. Finally, in April, 1951, Signor Mario Ricci publicly petitioned the Senate to stop the "insidious propaganda of the Protestant religion on the air," stating that it was offensive to the Catholic soul of the Italian people. For a while the quarter-hour services at 8:15 on Sunday morning were actually discontinued, but they were later resumed and now take place at 7:45.

There is no reason to suppose that the Vatican itself instigated Senator Ricci's protest, but on the other hand, no high Catholic prelate is known to have rebuked him for making it. A weak point in the Protestant case had been the fact that Sweden's state radio never permitted Roman Catholic broadcasts, but as noted in the preceding chapter this argument no longer pertains.

PROTESTANTISM PERSISTS

Despite discrimination, oppression, and outright persecution, the Waldensian Church in Italy, which actually antedates the Lutheran Reformation and is the oldest Protestant group of all, has slowly but surely spread southward—17 churches in 1848, 62 churches in 1950—through the principal cities of the peninsula. And it is just as Italian as spaghetti! In every generation since the twelfth century it has had martyrs to the Evangelical faith! The toll of Protestant lives has been incredibly high, and has kept the number of Waldensians correspondingly low.

Recently some American gospel missions have borne the brunt of violent anti-Protestant demonstrations because of their brash activity in the country districts and smaller towns, but they have also stirred a response in the people, especially at the bottom of the Boot. It is here also that there have been public disputations, organized by certain pastors with the cooperation of the priests, which are reported to have been conducted in a remarkable spirit of candor and good will.[1] By and large, however, the attitude of the Roman Church is one of bitter hostility to Protestant activity in Italy, which brings into the Waldensian Church 500 to 600 new converts yearly despite all sorts of sanctions.

The predicament of the Protestants in Spain is least enviable of all. Dr. John A. Mackay of Princeton Theological Seminary defines Spain as "a clerical state which maintains a Protestant ghetto." According to the Franco constitution, no one is to be molested for his religious beliefs or his private worship, but no public demonstrations nor ceremonies other than those of the Roman Catholic Church are allowed. Although the congregations meet loyally to worship and young men are being trained for the ministry, it can only be said that the 200 and more Evangelical parishes of Spain are still in the catacombs.

All Protestant schools have been closed since 1939. It is hardest of all for the young people, who must either dissemble their faith or automatically sacrifice all dreams of a higher education and a normal career, to say nothing of a marriage in their church and a public funeral at their death. Civil marriages are permissible only to those who can show documentary proof that they were not baptized in the Roman Catholic Church. By law a person who has

[1] In the spring of 1952, the Methodist young people of Rome arranged for a series of lectures on Roman Catholicism as a part of an ecumenical survey. Four outstanding representatives of Catholic Action accepted the invitation to speak in the Methodist Hall.

been baptized a Catholic finds it impossible to escape from the Roman Church. This is based on a treaty between the Vatican and the state. Yet the Protestant minority carries on and is growing.

This, then, is the status of Protestantism in an area of Europe where practically the only representative of the Christian faith is the Roman Church. In 1950 a conference of these Latin Evangelicals was called for the first time. It assembled under the auspices of the World Council of Churches at Torre Pellice in Italy for the purpose of exchanging information and comparing methods of work. The reports submitted at that time by the various delegations, consisting of outstanding pastors and laymen, indicated that the position of Evangelical Christians is anything but comfortable. The highest ambition of the older Protestant groups is not to convert all Catholics, or even a majority of them, but, firstly, to be able to preach the gospel freely by word and deed in their own countries and, secondly, to make such an impression upon the dominant church that it, too, will turn to the task of preaching the word of God effectively. In this postwar period they have less interest in trying to work up mass revivals and more interest in a working witness within the ordinary framework of daily life, in factory, mill, marketplace, school, and office.

Latin Protestants are terribly conscious of their numerical weakness. In view of the fact that nearly two-thirds of all European Catholics are found among those whose mother-tongues are rooted in the Latin language, can so little Evangelical leaven raise the whole loaf? What about this region and its religion?

THE CHURCH ON THE THRONE

There would be less cause to regret the plight of the heroic little Protestant churches in southern Europe if it could honestly be said that the Roman Church is using its vast power to meet the spiritual and social needs of the people whom it so tenaciously claims for its own. There might be some inclination to turn this statement against the state churches of the north and west, but I do not believe it is simply a Protestant prejudice to say that the parallel is not justified. In both instances, to be sure, there is a widespread indifference and even antagonism toward the church on the part of people who are supposed by law to be its members.[1] In both instances the churches have provided certain splendid examples of Christian social service and of elevated moral purpose. Reference has already been made, for instance—and will be made again—to the widely-heralded papal messages on social problems. But let's turn our attention for a moment from the churches to the sort of society that surrounds them.

A cursory description of generally prosperous conditions in Scandinavia has already been supplied and credit given both to Socialist policy and to the character of the people, not necessarily to the church. As one moves south, the picture changes. It does not matter much whether you take the two world wars into account or leave them out. Certain generalizations were as applicable to Europe in 1900 as they are today. Holland, Germany, Switzerland, and also Czechoslovakia, with their mixed Catholic-Protestant populations, have maintained high standards of living, education, and public welfare. In Belgium and France, where the population is nominally Roman Catholic but freedom of religion is an established fact, the picture becomes somewhat darker: educational standards are still very high, but public welfare falters and great gaps open between the rich and the poor. By the time you reach Italy and Spain, where Roman Catholicism sits enthroned, the contrast is so

---

[1] In the United States, incidentally, people of this class are largely outside the churches rather than inside, but just as indifferent or hostile. Yet most of them would resent being told they are not Christians.

marked that comparison with Scandinavian standards is impossible.

Undoubtedly, other factors than religion have—let me repeat— contributed to this state of affairs, but can the religious factor be entirely eliminated? In general, Scandinavia is no richer than Italy and Spain, which are also relatively poor in natural resources, yet the north enjoys prosperity, education, and stability, whereas the south is plagued with poverty, illiteracy, and simmering unrest.

Italy, for example, is chronically overpopulated, but this alone does not fully explain the poverty and lack of social progress, because the same general conditions prevailed in pre-Franco Spain, which was not over-populated. There is also a difference between Northern and Southern Italy. The North is far more industrialized, democratic, progressive, and tolerant than the South, where feudal landlords hold the peasants in virtual serfdom. Alone, the North with its average of 4 children per family might support itself, but it helps carry the South, where the average is 7 children.

Since World War II, Italy's unemployment figure hovers around the 2 million mark, but of course the number of persons affected is far larger. Governmental payrolls have been padded with redundant employees, such as the 1,300 people on the staff of the Ministry of Colonies, which has no colonies to administer.[1] Frantic efforts are still being made to export this surplus population to all parts of the world, but Italy's economic condition refuses to make any improvement.

THE VATICAN AND THE ITALIAN ELECTIONS

These things must be said to explain why Italy precariously hangs between communism and fascism. From an ideological viewpoint the average Italian is temperamentally unsuited to either

[1] See *The State of Europe,* by Howard Smith, Ch. XI, entitled, "Europe's Dead End Kid." London, Cresset Press, Ltd., 1950.

of these extremes, despite his buoyant delight in melodrama. Economic desperation, however, is a potent force.

Postwar Italy's major crisis came in the spring of 1948, on the occasion of the very first general election under her new constitution, just a few weeks after Czechoslovakia collapsed and was carried off by the Communists. A Red victory in Italy seemed assured and it looked as though a Soviet satellite would soon shine on the shores of the Mediterranean not too far from Malta, where Britain fought with all her might to turn the Nazi tide. There was public speculation about moving the Pope to Canada, if worse came to worst. Then in one frantic final burst of effort all possible resources were thrown into a last desperate struggle to preserve Italy for Western Europe.

Most of the credit for the ensuing victory undoubtedly goes to the downright and, technically speaking, illegal intervention of two outside powers, namely, the Vatican State and the United States.

The Vatican threw all of its weight behind the Christian Democratic Party of Alcide de Gasperi, a former Vatican librarian, by refusing Christian rites to professed Communists and by mobilizing the men of Catholic Action into political squads in 18,000 parishes. This organization alone claimed credit for getting out 40 per cent of the vote.

The role of America was quite openly publicized at that time by the fact that United States citizens of Italian origin were encouraged to send thousands of telegrams and letters to friends and relatives in the old country. Indeed, some misguided United States citizens in Italy endangered their American citizenship by entering the polls, also. More important was the almost daily announcement of some new concession to a democratic Italy—the return of Trieste, a gift of 29 merchant ships, restoration of Nazi "loot," Marshall Aid on the way, and even the statement that no Italian who was known to vote for the Communist Party would ever be granted a United States immigration visa. The cumulative effect was enormous. As a result, the Popular Front backed by the powerful Italian Communist Party—the largest in Western Europe —was held down to *only* 30 per cent of the vote in a country which is supposed to be 98 per cent Catholic.

Certain social reforms have been carried out by the Christian Democratic government since that time, but the unrest remains acute and not one major problem—employment, housing, public welfare, agricultural reform—has been fully tackled. Despite the outbreak of the Cold War, which gave many a Western Communist cold feet, the 1951 municipal elections revealed that the Red danger was far from past. Several large cities, it is true, lost the Communist regimes that had been in office since 1946, but in 27 provincial capitals the Reds took 37 per cent of the vote while the Christian Democrats dropped to 36.5 per cent.

Again the Roman Church had openly declared an anti-Catholic vote to be a mortal sin, but with less success. What was wrong? The Vatican paper confessed that not all baptized, or even practicing Catholics, were "faithful followers of the church." As a matter of fact, many Italian Communists go to church regularly! France and Italy are the nations with the largest Moscow followings in Western Europe. Can it be that the Roman Church has no other weapons except spiritual sanctions applied for political purposes?

Just before the local elections in the spring of 1952, the Pope issued an appeal based on the "intolerable" contrast between "offensive luxury" and "shameful poverty," urging the parish priests to get behind a civic program of social betterment. Is this to be taken with full seriousness or is it merely election propaganda? There is little or no indication that the Roman Church is actually leading the way toward a new society by its own example. On the other hand, it is plain that the political crisis is not yet past, as the following paragraph plainly indicates:

The Vatican, a tiny independent state in the western neighborhoods of Rome, has taken an intense part. Each night for more than a week before the elections the Vatican radio has been leading Catholics in the recitation of the Rosary. The Reverend Riccardo Lombardi, speaking from the same station, has warned Catholics that "the shame of a Communist mayor in Rome" is so grave a danger that abstention from voting will be a mortal sin, an offense grave enough to deny the offender entrance into heaven after death unless forgiven before then.[1]

NEITHER COMMUNISTS NOR PROTESTANTS IN SPAIN!

Unfortunately space does not permit even a sketchy description of what has happened in Spain during the past twenty years. But it is *not* voting Communist. Franco has turned time back with a vengeance. Every radical and almost every liberal element in the country has been exterminated or rendered helpless. In medieval style the nobility, the army, and the church still run the state. Spain and Portugal are the only countries in Europe without compulsory elementary schooling, and the illiteracy rate (over 60 per cent) soars above that of the rest of Europe. The Roman Church in Spain is in charge of all primary education, exercises a final censorship on the public press, owns tremendous areas of land, receives large subsidies from the public treasury, flouts every human freedom in its effort to preserve its religious monopoly.

Papal encyclicals of which the Spanish hierarchy disapproves are not published in Spain. In fact, the Spanish hierarchy sturdily rebutted the Vatican's suggestion that a Christian press should be used to educate the people, not oppress them. As a parish paper in

[1] "Local Elections in Italy," by Barrett McGurn, in the *New York Herald Tribune* (Paris Edition) May 23, 1952.

Saragossa said in 1948, "People who talk about liberty are childish, for why should Spain adopt the habits of other countries?" [1]

Spain has always occupied a proud Catholic position because of her long resistance to the Moslem conquest of Europe, her spectacular era of discovery that carried the cross around the world, and her ruthless inquisition to root out heresy. Spanish Catholics, because of the part their ancestors played in the Crusades, are not required to observe meatless Fridays, although this dispensation has been withdrawn gradually from all Spain's former colonies. Even prouder than the Spanish hierarchy, however, are the Basques of the northwest corner of the country, descendants of the inhabitants who successfuly repulsed the representatives of the notorious Inquisition in the sixteenth century.

In 1951 a group of priests addressed a letter to their bishop insisting that the Franco regime be exposed for its corruption and tyranny. The letter was a strong plea for freedom to assemble, freedom of speech, and freedom of thought. It was the old cry of Don Carlos echoing again on the twentieth century stage and not merely from Schiller. But nothing was said about freedom for non-Catholics, too.

It must be said that American Catholic voices have not been entirely silent in this debate, and for their pains they have been roundly rebuked in Spain. Cardinal Segura of Seville, who is largely responsible for the recent wave of attacks on Protestants, published a letter in March, 1952, wherein he said:

We are not surprised to know that there are Catholics who proclaim religious freedom for all as a divine ideal, as well as Protestants making the same mistake, and that they are demanding of us Spaniards a similar liberty as payment in advance for their favors (namely, foreign

[1] Quoted by W. E. Garrison, series of four articles on Spain in *The Christian Century*, November, 1950.

loans). They do not realize that this demand would, the religious situation in Spain being what we know it to be, run counter to Divine Law. We pray God that both may eventually become convinced of this undeniable truth, or at any rate of the fact that we regard it as such. . . . Spain can in no wise allow the Protestants the same rights as Catholics in the public practice and profession of their beliefs.

Two months later the magazine *Ecclesia* charged American Catholic writers with "doctrinal errors contrary to papal encyclicals," probably because they were influenced more by political philosophy than by theology. In reply, the editor of *America,* the best known Catholic periodical in the United States, stated that while he did not regard Cardinal Segura's position as untenable, he felt that it was not the only possible position that good Catholics could take.

Lest there be any temptation to assume that the Spanish Catholics are acting on principles that perhaps the Vatican does not approve, let us look at a few stipulations contained in the Concordat of 1851 (which was publicly reaffirmed on February 12, 1952, by the Bureau of Diplomatic Information of the Foreign Office in Madrid) as summarized by Paul Hutchinson in *The New Leviathan.*

Catholicism is to be the sole religion, all others being excluded; the church shall have control over all education and Catholicism shall be taught in all schools; the government shall accord all honors to bishops and Catholic clergy and shall support them in all their efforts against the perversion of the faith of the people; the government shall not interfere in any way with the bishops or clergy in enforcing ecclesiastical discipline. . . . All public officials and members of the armed forces must attend mass; all prisoners, including the thousands who still rot in prison after capture in the civil war, must attend mass; publication or circulation of the Bible is prohibited.[1]

[1] P. 132. Chicago, Willett, Clark and Co., 1946.

THE NEW ROMAN EMPIRE

There is no doubt that the Roman Catholic Church, although it contains within itself a perplexing variety of apparent contradictions, stands united against the rest of the world. This unity is a mixture of the geographical, the physical, and the spiritual. That it contains spiritual power is undeniable, but Catholicism's chief power resides in its claim to universality and its possession of a magnificent capital, which is located in a tiny principality (108 acres) on the banks of the Tiber in Italy, called the Vatican State.[1] The chief of this state is the pope, the successor to St. Peter, the vicar of Christ on earth, and the head of a church that lays exaggerated claim to 350 million adherents.

The Roman Catholic Church is in many European and South American countries a state church, but in its totality as represented by the Holy See it is a church state. It has never surrendered its claim to temporal power, which was lost in 1870 but technically restored by Mussolini in 1929 when the Vatican State was established. Basically, it is a totalitarian state that lays totalitarian claims upon the world. From a Christian point of view—aside from its dictatorial implications—the concept is a magnificent ideal; in reality, the church of Christ has not shown itself to be immune from the social and political diseases that accompany even a benevolent tyranny.

What is the Vatican from which the state takes its name? It is the official residence of the pope, who is also the Catholic bishop of

---

[1] Its wealth is enormous. Howard Smith, in *The State of Europe*, p. 262, reports that the Vatican alone has a controlling interest in 31 Italian industries and minority holdings in banks, shipping companies, insurance firms, mines, textile and hydroelectric industries. It also has extensive foreign holdings in enterprises such as banks, publishing houses, and mills in France, Belgium, Holland, the United States, and other countries, estimated at a total world figure of 240 million dollars. This is big business.

Rome. It is a palace adjoining St. Peter's Cathedral on the north. In many devout minds it far outranks the importance of all other earthly capitals. In it are not only libraries and museums, but also dozens of offices for the transaction of papal business. A vast network of communications keeps it in close touch with all parts of the world. It hopes soon to have, in addition to its railroad station, a merchant fleet flying the Vatican flag and perhaps an airport of its own near Rome. Recently, the ground for a new broadcasting station was procured from the Italian Government, its acreage being ten times that of the Vatican State itself.

This grandeur and prestige have been regained only rather recently. Time after time in Roman history the pope's authority has been flaunted and defied until his influence became negligible and the Holy See little more than a Roman bishopric. One hundred and fifty years ago this state of affairs prevailed, but Napoleon, in the hope of using the world-wide church to further his own imperial interests, invested the papal office with fresh significance by recognizing its territorial claims. Mussolini—as the quotation at the head of the chapter implies—followed exactly the same misguided policy 120 years later. Pius VII, while taking advantage of Bonaparte's favor, refused to be used as the short-lived Emperor's tool and had the pleasure of seeing the Congress of Vienna in 1815 confirm his new holdings in Central Italy. But in 1870, within a few days of the proclamation of papal infallibility, these possessions, an area of 16,000 square miles—about one-half the size of Maine or South Carolina—fell to the new Kingdom of Italy. For the next sixty years, until the treaty with the Duce, the popes considered themselves prisoners in Italy.

Today the Holy See ("seat" or "diocese") exercises its spiritual, moral, and political influence on the modern world in a variety of ways. Something of its spiritual influence was vividly demonstrated during the Holy Year pageantry of 1950 at Rome, which gave all Roman Catholic Christians outside the Russian orbit an impressive token of world-wide solidarity in the face of global Communist aggression. Several very important proclamations were issued during the year, all of which tended to rivet the eyes and ears of the faithful on Rome as the final source of truth in every area of life.

Time and again the indisputable authority of Catholic doctrine was emphasized, not only against the multitudinous secular "isms" of the world but also, in the 1950 Christmas Message, against all attempts to establish contact with the other churches of Christendom. There is only one true church and the only road to unity is the road of return to the bosom of the mother church. The possibility that the Word of God might sometimes be distorted or even betrayed by the very church that tries to keep it pure was rigidly excluded. Rome is always right! "The priest is another Christ" was written into the Holy Year *Admonitions to the Clergy,* and soon this slogan appeared on public posters in Spain depicting the figure of a priest behind whom Christ was dimly seen.

ROME BUTTRESSES ITS CLAIM TO INFALLIBILITY

Toward the end of the Holy Year a new dogma was proclaimed that nullified much of the favorable impression that this united front had made even on Europe's divided Protestants: namely, the Dogma of the Assumption—the bodily ascent of the Virgin Mary into heaven. It was not based primarily on theological research or Biblical evidence, but on what was referred to as the cumulative Catholic conviction of many centuries. As Pope Pius himself indicated, the voice of the people is the voice of God.

The unanimous reaction in the Protestant world—in addition to a shocked denial of the doctrine itself—was that the gulf within Christendom had opened wider, just at a time when the voice of all Christian people seemed to be clamoring for a firmer fellowship regardless of differences. The new dogma promptly put an end to persistent hopes that the Vatican might be preparing itself to negotiate an equitable basis of cooperation with non-Roman churches.

The earlier launching of a *una sancta* movement in which other churches were invited to participate seemed to be a step in the right direction, except for the fact that it was to be 85 per cent Catholic. By the end of the Holy Year, both the Roman and non-Roman churches seemed to have abandoned all thought of joining in common cause. The Bishop of Rome split Christendom in 1054, when the Eastern, or Orthodox, Church became separated from the West, and the Vatican remains today—contrary to popular myth—one of the greatest divisive forces in the world.

It must not be thought, however, that there are no chinks in the totalitarian front of the Roman Church. Despite the papal injunction against it, there are still numerous semi-official contacts between Protestants and Catholics.

Some Catholic scholars are obviously deeply interested in the ecumenical movement of Protestant and Orthodox churches and cautiously preserve a friendly attitude toward inter-church fellowship. They are not wholly convinced that Rome is entirely right and that everybody else is entirely wrong. Some have the courage to speak a good word for Luther, Calvin, and the Protestant reliance on the Word of God alone. In the fall of 1951 a group of forty French Catholics broke with Rome completely on the ground of its religious totalitarianism. Wherever priests and pastors were driven together in common defense against Hitlerism there is still to be found a warmth of mutual esteem and Christian friendship. In many areas the local Protestant-Catholic relationships have never been better.

By and large, however, the Vatican has no sympathy for such

manifestations of fellowship, especially since the Protestant churches refused to be recruited in the Catholic crusade against communism. More will be said about this in the final chapter.

The statements of the Vatican on moral issues and social questions, despite their Roman aberrations, are important declarations of Christian conviction on many of the basic issues of our time. Therefore, they merit more study than they usually receive. All too often Catholics simply pay lip service to them, whereas non-Catholics brush them aside as nothing more than a subtle form of Roman propaganda. Actually, they should serve as the basis of serious discussion.

A group of Oxford scholars (non-Catholics) have devoted considerable time to an analysis of the important social encyclicals from 1891 to 1945 and have come to the conclusion that they are neither so clear nor so consistent as the dogma of papal infallibility would lead one to expect. Regarding the question of private property, the statements begin with an outright condemnation of all attempts by the state to transfer ownership (thus putting the interest of the family above those of the state) but conclude with the explicit approval—forty years later—of the principle that "certain forms of property must be reserved to the state, since they carry with them a power too great to be left to private individuals." The two positions are not in themselves mutually exclusive, inasmuch as the first one champions the family (but also capitalism) against the state, whereas the second champions society against the individual, but the second encyclical had to admit that "since the time of Leo XIII important changes have taken place both in the economic regime and in socialism." The Vatican deserves more credit for changing its position than for trying to be unchangeable. Of what particular value is a reputation for infallibility?

The question as to whether further modifications of the papal position may not be necessary is raised by the violent reaction following the Pope's speech to a meeting of Italian obstetricians in October, 1951, in which he said that "to save the mother's life is a very noble aim, but the direct killing of the baby as a means to that end is not permitted." This was nothing new, but a storm of protest arose. Could non-Catholic mothers trust Roman Catholic doctors? The following month the Pope amplified the statement in an effort to soften it, and laid heavy emphasis on the word "direct," but basic doctrine has not yet been altered.

Roman teaching admits, for example, that sexual intercourse may have "secondary ends, such as the cultivation of mutual love and the quieting of concupiscence," but these secondary ends may not be satisfied where the fulfillment of the primary end—procreation—is inadvisable, to say nothing of countenancing any form of family control for social or economic reasons. It can probably be assumed that all people who call themselves Christian would rather increase the total number of jobs and the total supply of food than employ birth control as the solution of social and economic problems, but here again the Roman Catholic Church—South Italy being within a stone's throw of every high-flown encyclical!—is open to suspicion that its motives in advocating unlimited procreation are tinged with religious self-interest. Protestant Europe asks: What has the Vatican done for Italy?

THE VATICAN AND POWER POLITICS

Most significant for our times are the Vatican's political activities. Where does the church leave off and where does the state begin? Its international behavior leaves an open question: namely, whether the Holy See is primarily concerned with the salvation of all men and the welfare of society, or whether it is not chiefly interested in the extension of its own ecclesiastical empire.

The Oxford scholars, in their study of papal statements against communism, observe that there "seems to be a tendency of the Roman Church to judge governments according to whether they help or hinder the church considered as an organization, without reference to broader issues of Christian morality." In short, it fails to see that all totalitarianism—its own included—is at bottom identical. The totalitarianism of Catholicism appears in at least two principles: absolute submission to the Roman pontiff and absolute freedom for the Roman Church. What this latter freedom implies becomes quite clear in the Spanish concordat.[1]

Catholicism, as an ecclesiastical power that finds an enemy in Stalin and an ally in Franco, expresses its convictions politically. In several places it has been instrumental in turning back the Communist tide, but in no instance has it achieved more than a temporary political victory. In European states where communism came to power there has been individual resistance and even martyrdom, but in France and Italy—to say nothing of Poland, Czechoslovakia, and Hungary—the threat of automatic excommunication (issued formally and publicly in 1949) has had little or no perceptible effect on the trend of events. In fact, the church behind the Iron Curtain has suffered serious repercussions from the Vatican statements, as a consequence of which a change of policy toward communism (similar to the one regarding socialism?) is being considered in Vatican circles: namely, an endeavor to obtain as much protection as possible for the Catholics in East Europe through pressure in diplomatic and political channels.[2]

[1] For further papal pronouncements, especially on the subject of democracy, separation of church and state, and religious liberty, see Pope Leo XIII's *Immortale Dei*, published in 1885. It refers directly to the principles upon which American democracy is based.

[2] For evidence of this change of approach observe the papal message to the Russian people in late summer 1952, containing an attempt to divide the people from the regime.

In this connection, it is reported that the conduct of the Vatican's foreign affairs is to be placed in the hands of a committee of nine cardinals and that a new corps of priest-diplomats is to be trained for foreign service. Evidently, it is felt that the Vatican's postwar activities on the broad terrain of international negotiations has paid off. In the eyes of many Catholics this politicking is as suspect as it is to Protestants, but, as in the case of the recently proclaimed dogma, the voice of the Pope on all matters affecting the new Roman empire will probably turn out to be the voice of the people.

It would take us too far afield even to comment on this international aspect of Roman Catholic policy, in which the proposed appointment of an American ambassador to the Vatican unquestionably plays a major part. All the countries of Western Europe, except for Scandinavia and Switzerland (although there is a papal nuncio at Berne), now have full diplomatic relations. A United States appointment would give the Vatican the right to replace the apostolic delegate in Washington with a nuncio, not only to deal with the civil government about international affairs but also to provide one central headquarters for the Roman Catholic Church in America. In the long run these diplomatic posts have probably proved to be more effective instruments of Roman policy than the "Christian" political parties that are invariably to be found in European countries and from which even the local Catholic authorities—to say nothing of the Vatican—obviously must dissociate themselves, at least where the façade of non-interference needs to be preserved.

This does not mean that Catholic political parties as such will be abandoned, even when they tend to aggravate religious differences and split the country. They are the national expression of Roman public policy, and therefore, they will continue to be an acute embarrassment to the Protestants who face the dilemma of trying to organize parties of their own, or letting the Roman Catholics—as Catholics—gradually gain full political ascendancy.

Early in 1952, the Protestant President of the West German Bundestag pleaded with Catholics to pay due regard to parity and not to arouse Protestant resentment by their more intense political activity. He has also told Protestants that their political weakness is their own fault. The Christian Democrats in Germany had started out bravely after the last war as an interconfessional party, but the experienced Catholics of the old Zentrum Partei have long since left the less experienced Protestants far behind.

WHAT IF THE CHURCH GAINS THE WORLD . . .?

It is apparent that the Roman Catholic Church has sustained terrible losses of prestige and political power in Eastern Europe as a result of Communist aggression. Lithuania, Poland, Czechoslovakia, and Hungary were Roman Catholic countries run, by and large, according to Catholic policy. Great influence was wielded also in Rumania—through the Uniat Church, which has since transferred allegiance to Moscow—and Yugoslavia, too, where there is no doubt that the Catholic Croats played the Nazi game against the Serbian Orthodox. In any assessment of present strength in the struggle for control of Europe, the Pope has lost these "divisions," and he stands to lose still more if, for example, American economic support were to be withdrawn from Southern Europe.

Italy, which was rescued once, could still go Communist. France—from the viewpoint of Catholic loyalty and regardless of Communist strength—can only be described as lukewarm toward papal political problems. Therefore, while it is true that Western Europe is governed almost exclusively by a mixture of Roman Catholics and Socialists, and the prime minister in virtually every country south of Scandinavia is Catholic, the Vatican State *as a temporal power* is actually a very flimsy structure built largely on diplomatic finesse rather than spiritual power.

Perhaps this great interconfessional predicament can best be summed up by saying that the Protestants of Europe are just as interested as Roman Catholics in world peace, but they do not believe, in the words of the 1950 Christmas Message, that the dove of peace can settle with confidence only at the side of the Holy Father. They do not believe that wars would cease if Catholic doctrine were universally practiced. It is difficult to imagine that the Vatican within reach of its own historical archives believes that.

Protestants do believe, however, that the Roman Catholic Church could become the most powerful single agency in the world for a Christian order of society if it would abandon its political ambitions based on the hunger for temporal power and become simply a church founded on Peter's confession, not only that Jesus is Christ but that "I am a sinful man." To Catholics this may sound naive, but to European Protestants—especially the Latin Protestants—it makes sense. The trouble is that Rome cannot effect this change without, literally, ceasing to be the Rome of the Caesars, the Rome of Constantine, the Rome of the Middle Ages, and the Rome of the Renaissance, all of which have taken the church captive.

According to legend, Christ himself came to the edge of the pagan city, when it seemed that Peter would flee. Peter, ashamed, turned back to die. The legendary footprints of Jesus are still to be seen outside the walls in a musty, dusty, neglected little chapel, whereas Peter sits, through no will of his own, on a golden throne in the world's most magnificent church, where his toe may be kissed by pilgrims.

7

Christian Faith in Mortal Combat

When we see disagreement between history and dogma, we must first ask ourselves: Do we correctly understand dogma? —Metropolitan Sergius, 1935.

Separation of church and state signifies neither that the church stands outside the state nor that it is a state inside the state.—Bulgarian Foreign Minister, 1949.

THE Iron Curtain fell in grooves well greased for it. That "East is East and West is West" is nothing new in Europe, for there has always been a difference here, and the dividing line today cuts *more or less* where it has always cut. Novel and portentous only is the startling fact that Western Europe now stretches as far as San Francisco, and Eastern Europe spreads across Siberia to Vladivostok. Usually it is said that America and Russia face each other on the Elbe, which is a much more commonplace—and typically European!—way of expressing the same idea.

If you draw a rough line down across the map of Europe from the Baltic Sea on the north to the Adriatic on the south, you will find that history has already hung several curtains on it. It would be too much to say that any of them ever really separated Europe from Asia; within Europe they parted East from West. However, when the most recent curtain is added to these laminated draperies, which originally offered no special obstacle to the prewar tourist but were tough to tear, the result is more than a last layer of waterproof shellac. It becomes a wall of iron, thanks to the Red Army.

What are these other curtains? The first is ethnic. So far we have dealt with Anglo-Saxons, the Nordic and the Latin peoples, but south and east of Berlin and east of Trieste begins a Slavic world where Wends, Poles, Czechs, Slovaks, Slovenes, Croats, and Serbs speak closely related languages. The second curtain is economic: industry, big business, sophisticated cities are replaced by agriculture, handicraft, and unpaved villages. The third curtain is social: feudal differences between great landowners and the peasants became increasingly obvious. The fourth curtain is political: the tocsin of the French Revolution—liberty and equality—was much less audible than the muezzin from a nearby Turkish minaret. The fifth curtain is religious: tonsured, medieval Roman Catholicism seems almost modern to the Western traveler in the presence of bearded Eastern Orthodoxy of the fourth century.

Most generalizations are false at some point, and the paragraph above is so full of possible exceptions—Czechoslovakia, for example!—that it would seem to contain no truth at all. But it does. No tourist can move steadily eastward through Europe from Belgium to Bulgaria without noting these changes. The transitions are not always sudden nor dramatic, but they are there.

Of course, there are radical differences among the Eastern states, too. Briefly, these differences are derived from the tidal deposits of the surging East-West forces. Some nations were marked, like Bulgaria and Serbia, by the Turkish Empire that pushed to the gates of Vienna in the sixteenth century and did not wholly recede from the Balkans until shortly before World War I. There are plenty of Moslems left in Bulgaria and Yugoslavia. Other East European nations, like Latvia and Estonia, were molded by contact with the Teutonic Knights from the West, who subdued and occupied the Baltic area, from which their last descendants were evacuated by Hitler in the midst of World War II.

To take another set of formative forces, the Protestant Reformation influenced the regions closest to Germany and Sweden, which, by the way, knew its greatest era of expansion at that time. The Roman Catholic Counter-Reformation, on the other hand, moved northward from Italy into the Austro-Hungarian area, which today is 80 per cent Catholic.

Those regions nearest to Constantinople, however, remained loyal to the Orthodox faith. Thus was the multi-colored pattern of Eastern Europe woven intricately on the loom of historical religion. Its people possessed a rich culture of their own, but by West European standards they seemed to be economically underdeveloped, socially retarded, and politically immature. The fact that they were probably Europe's happiest and most hospitable people is, in this world, a fact of less importance!

Signs of social and economic progress were abundant, but things were moving much too slowly to prevent the entire area from falling prey to outside leadership. In geopolitical parlance, the whole region was a power vacuum, and Russia filled it. Today, of course, the ordinary tourist cannot travel from Brussels even so far as Budapest, and by the same token this book cannot pursue the even tenor of its way around the continent. We would like to take the roofs off those Eastern churches and politely look inside. Instead of that we are compelled to peek and squint through whatever tiny openings we can find.

Contacts between the churches East and West in Europe are today as rare as messages between the enemies in World War II. It is not only difficult to learn how the churches are faring under the Communists, but it is impossible to erect any standard of comparison with the Christian situation in the West. Consequently, some Westerners give the Eastern churches up for lost; others imagine that practically the only vital Christian witness left in Europe is to be found behind the Iron Curtain.

As a matter of fact, it is evident that there are vast differences among the Iron Curtain countries themselves. If you include the Soviet zones of Germany and Austria, there are at least three distinct areas. News of church life in Germany and Austria is plentiful and practically complete, because the churches themselves have not yet really been divided by the Iron Curtain. It may happen any day. But news from the satellite states ceased to be either plentiful or reliable in 1948 and 1949. News from Russia itself, including the Baltic states and other annexed areas, is exceedingly rare and highly unreliable. In fact, there are only two authentic Eastern European countries that are fully accessible to study because they are still outside the Russian orbit: namely, Greece and Yugoslavia. Perhaps it might be just as well to begin with them.

GREECE AND YUGOSLAVIA—OUTSIDE THE IRON CURTAIN

Greece is a non-Slavic but almost wholly Orthodox country that has, with Western help but at exorbitant cost, escaped both communism and Russian domination. Nearly 8 million Greeks belong to the national church, less than 50,000 to the Roman and Protestant groups. Over 800 Orthodox churches were destroyed and 600 priests killed in the course of the war. In 4 postwar years, 270 priests were murdered by Communist guerrillas, 800 villages were destroyed, and 2,800 children were carried away. Today, a shaken and saddened church is trying to set its people's feet firmly in the way of physical and spiritual revival. Renewal and evangelism are integral parts of its religious program, as well as an amazing variety of community activities designed to lift the social and economic level of the parishes. They have a long way to go.

One remarkable aspect of this established church, which is divided into 65 dioceses, is that the largest parishes contain no more than 3,000 families, whereas the smaller ones range from only 50 to 500 families. As noted in Chapter Two, there are signs of new Christian life in the branches of this venerable old tree, but its dense shadow still prevents the unimpeded growth of other communions. Time and again, the freedom of minorities has been transgressed and even though the Greek Government is sometimes hostile toward the state church, it is unlikely that the Orthodox will voluntarily advocate full freedom for all.

Those of the Greek Orthodox faith believe as firmly as do the Roman Catholics that theirs is the one true church, but, after prolonged study and prayer, it was decided to join in the ecumenical fellowship of the World Council of Churches. The Orthodox claim to be the *una sancta* finds no dubious echo in worldly ambitions to outshine Rome, as was plainly demonstrated in planning the great festival to celebrate the nineteen-hundredth anniversary of St. Paul's arrival in Europe. Visitors from representative Christian churches all over the world were invited in June, 1951, to join in a pilgrimage, not to glorify a living churchman, but to retrace the missionary steps of St. Paul himself as he traveled through Greece on foot and by boat. The Vatican declined to accept this invitation because the Greek Government had not given permission to the Holy See to establish a papal representative in Athens. In reply, the Greeks pointed out that the nature of the St. Paul Festival was religious, not political.

Yugoslavia, while completely Communist, is—like Greece—outside the Iron Curtain, but Slavic. Religiously speaking, it can be divided roughly into two parts: the Roman Catholic North and the Orthodox South, which have opposed each other bitterly for hundreds of years. A hundred and fifty thousand Protestants are scattered mainly through the northern half of the country among Slovak, Hungarian, and German-speaking minorities. No church escaped the first onslaught of Tito's anti-religious attack, but it must not be forgotten that these attacks had political overtones. In other words, no group was openly persecuted for its religious beliefs. The Orthodox leadership was charged with reaction and treated accordingly; the Roman Catholic Croats were charged with Fascist collaboration, and their Archbishop Stepinac was sentenced to prison, from which he was subsequently released; many Protestants were interned or fled the country for a variety of reasons ranging from collaboration with the Nazis to a determination to seek economic and political freedom elsewhere.

Of far greater interest to us just now is the fact that the restoration of a considerable degree of freedom to the religious bodies, including the resumption of their Western contacts, coincided with Marshal Tito's defiance of Soviet Russia. What did the first visitors find? The church that had, of course, been separated from the state, was materially in a seriously weakened condition, but religion was flourishing vigorously among the people. Churches today are crowded with worshipers, and both pastors and priests are desperately trying to satisfy the spiritual thirst of thousands of eager members. Sequestrated church buildings have gradually been restored to religious use and theological seminaries expanded for the training of ministers.

The tension between church and state is rapidly relaxing, although a Ministry of Religious Affairs keeps a close eye on all church matters. This does not mean that the separation of church and state will not be rigorously pursued by the state. Notice was served early in 1952 that the three theological faculties would be eliminated from public universities the following autumn, but that the church was free to establish its own institutions and might even hope for some financial help from the state.

The problem now becomes one of finance in a country that is struggling with the problem of rebuilding 1,400 destroyed churches. Furthermore, there is active anti-religious propaganda even in the elementary schools, designed to separate children from the faith of their parents. Teachers are required each month to report what they have done to combat "mysticism" and to discourage such things as the observance of religious holidays, prayers, and Bible study.

Marshal Tito himself leaves no doubt as to the official attitude. In May, 1952, he went on record with the public statement that Yugoslav youths were to become "new men." Referring to accusations from the West that Yugoslav children were systematically being alienated from the church and from God, he said, "We cannot agree to a people surrendering to superstition. We do not persecute religion, but we must fight against superstition." No doubt a certain admixture of superstition is to be found in the popular exercise of any form of faith. On the other hand, it is a known fact that convinced Communists like Tito consider Christianity to be nothing but a bundle of superstitions. In short, the race is on between Christians and atheists to see who will, in the long run, retain hold on the Yugoslav state and its people.

One month after the above-cited statement, there was a brief meeting between the Marshal and the Serbian Patriarch Vikentji. The Patriarch thanked the Marshal in behalf of the church, and the Marshal said, "The Federal Government will, as it has done hitherto, adopt an attitude of correctness regarding all constructive work by the church for the maintenance and strengthening of the brotherhood and unity of the Serbian people, its freedom and independence, and the development of Yugoslavia." At the present time, this type of lopsided struggle with ill-concealed hostility corresponds to the East European idea of religious liberty.

The Union of Orthodox Priests dating from 1889 and dedicated to the task of fostering both the material and spiritual interests of the clergy has helped to re-establish contacts with the government. Over 1,600 out of 2,300 priests and monks belong to it, and most of them have shown their loyalty to the present regime by joining the Popular Front, also. In 1951 two bishops of the church formally attended the union's annual meeting for the first time, implying that the Holy Synod is ready to cooperate with the union, although it has never been officially recognized.

Priests are now eligible for state social insurance as employees of their religious communities. Nearly 100 Orthodox priests are employed in government positions and twice as many more in various social and humanitarian agencies, presumably imparting a Christian emphasis to public welfare activities. Church leaders are now able to visit Western Europe and the United States, and, unlike the representatives of the Soviet satellite states, they seem to be able to avoid the use of hackneyed Cominform terminology.

The Protestant minorities (110,000 Lutherans, 35,000 Reformed, 3,000 Baptists, 2,300 Methodists, 2,700 United Brethren, and others) are generally recognized for the first time as indigenous churches. Out of their common needs the various groups have mutually assisted one another in the common use of church buildings and pastoral services. Even the Orthodox priests are frequently involved in this interchange. A new Lutheran federation has been formed and publicly recognized by the Orthodox Church as well as by the state.

No church schools are permitted under the new regime, but Sunday schools and confirmation classes are held regularly. In some areas even the Serbian Orthodox are venturing into the field of parish education for the first time. In Slovenia 95 per cent of all Protestant school children study their catechisms twice weekly on a released time basis and the pastors are reimbursed by the state for this instruction, despite the fact that the schoolteachers are paid to discourage religion. To top it off, the Yugoslav Republic issued a postage stamp commemorating the four-hundredth anniversary of the publication of the Lutheran Primer in 1551, the first book printed in the Slovene language.

It might be considered inexcusably flippant to say that a touch of communism may in the long run do the whole religious situation in Yugoslavia less harm than good, but there are those who feel keenly that the entire Christian church stands in need of a radical shock treatment, provided that it is not permanently twisted from the gospel to serve some political or ideological end. Developments in Yugoslavia, as contrasted with the other Communist states, are worth watching closely.

BETWEEN TWO IRON CURTAINS

A satellite is a planet revolving around a sun. The satellite states of East Europe travel in a fixed orbit around the USSR. Travel is not a very good word, because the vast majority of their inhabitants are frozen fast. They cannot move into Russia except as prisoners, nor away from it except as refugees. Most people, incidentally, do not relish the idea of being either prisoners or refugees, which accounts for the ultimate acquiescence of the average man to the forces of circumstance beyond his control. Caught between two Iron Curtains, therefore, these people and their countries are rapidly being revamped along Soviet lines. It is hardly likely that their distinctive characteristics will long survive an intensive leveling process, but religious differences perhaps have as good a chance as any. What impact has the new order had on their Christian life?

You will recall that in spite of the influence of Eastern Orthodoxy in the southeast and of Protestantism in the northwest, the Communist countries of East Europe—owing to big majorities in Poland, Czechoslovakia, and Hungary—are predominantly Roman Catholic. Eastern Europe contained 45 million Roman Catholics (nearly 25 per cent of the European total and many of the most devout) as compared with 25 million Orthodox (outside of Russia) and only a few million Protestants.[1]

Refugees by the hundreds of thousands have fled from the sinking satellites, but needless to say the vast majority of the original populations, insofar as they were not actually driven away, stayed where they were. Having once elected to stay, they had to make the best of it. Relatively few of them, even among the clergy, remained because they were acutely conscious of a special duty to themselves, to their country, and to their church. When subjected to a series of minor decisions, the average family unit will usually continue to give personal possessions precedence over political or even religious principles.

In the light of the Catholic figures and the general circumstances, it is understandable that the Vatican felt impelled to launch a crusade against the Kremlin to try to rescue the souls of its faithful. In the light of the same statistics, plus the persistent pretensions of the Roman Catholic Church as a temporal state, it is equally understandable why the Communists are determined to break its power.

When the Pope in 1949 tried to meet the growing menace by ordering priests to withhold the sacraments from all Catholics who so much as read a Communist paper, the governments of Poland

[1] We should also keep in mind Albania, a very small country with a population 70 per cent Moslem.

and Czechoslovakia countered immediately by declaring it illegal for a priest to excommunicate anyone for political reasons. The average Christian being anything but a martyr, Catholic priests found it utterly impossible to obey the Pope in Rome and continue to live behind the Iron Curtain. How serious the conflicts of conscience really were is difficult to ascertain, but, as was indicated in the previous chapter, the excommunication order was allowed to lapse and a new strategy was sought.

Rome, however, certainly did not approve the concordat concluded in 1950 between the Polish state and the Polish Catholic Church. This seems to be the only full and formal agreement of its kind in any of the satellite states. Naturally, it is full of concessions and compromises, whereby the state permits unrestricted religious instruction in the schools, complete freedom of worship, including pilgrimages and processions, and subsidizes the church in various ways. The bishops, for their part, undertake to support the social revolution, defend the claims of Poland to the western territories taken after the war, and to recognize the limitations of the Pope's authority to the realm of faith, morals, and ecclesiastical jurisdiction. Of Poland alone can it be said that the Catholic Church has succeeded in wresting important temporary advantages from a Communist state.

There is no disguising the fact that, although the bright flames of a genuine struggle for religious liberty can occasionally be seen through the smoke of the Christian-Communist controversy in Eastern Europe, the real object of the battle is a new relationship between church and state. Only rarely does the battle seem to rage around a new relationship to society, to the people themselves. Here we encounter again precisely the same essential problem that has dogged our footsteps from the British Isles to Scandinavia and down to Latin Europe; namely, the inability of the Christian witness in the last years to furnish some practical guidance toward the reordering of society. More than anywhere else, this question haunts and taunts the devout Christians of Eastern Europe as they see the Old World being deliberately demolished and a new one erected from which the church is clearly excluded.

SEPARATING CHURCH FROM STATE, BUT NOT STATE FROM CHURCH

Following Russia's example, the satellite states (and Yugoslavia) have written the separation of church and state into their new constitutions. But—in contrast to the idea of separation in France or the United States—it is a one-way separation only. While preventing the church from exercising any influence on the state, the state—being totalitarian—retains an effective control over every public expression of church life! Exactly as in Catholic Spain, the basic assumption is that religious freedom prevails as long as *reasonable* provision is made for the private worship of those who insist on retaining *unreasonable* religious views.

It is safe to say that all three faiths—Orthodox, Roman Catholic, and Protestant—are unanimous in agreeing that this kind of liberty behind the Iron Curtain is tantamount to persecution, but it must not be assumed that all three faiths agree in what they would prefer to see. No doubt, the Orthodox would like to enjoy the status of established national churches federated under the spiritual leadership of the Moscow patriarch, the Roman Catholics would obviously prefer full state-church privileges protected by a Vatican agreement, whereas most Protestants would be satisfied with freedom of conscience and autonomy with or without official state recognition and support.

What is the present working relation of church to state in the satellite states? A major touchstone of this question is, as usual,

financial. In all cases the new regime—to everybody's astonishment
—continued, wherever it was customary, to supply the salaries of
the clergy, maintain church property (which sooner or later became state property), subsidize theological schools, and, in general,
pay the nation's religious bills. In some cases, payments were
delayed or temporarily withheld, thus giving good grounds for
suspecting that the Communists had discovered the use of an effective weapon for weakening or totally disarming any potential
Christian opposition. Such tactics met with considerable success in
Bulgaria early in 1948. When Exarch Stefan I finally resigned,
regular payments were resumed, but constant financial pressure
has steadily undermined all attempts of the Orthodox Church to
maintain its position on questions of principle.

In Hungary the Protestant and Catholic churches have a formal
understanding with the regime that state support will decline
gradually and cease entirely in twenty years. Meanwhile, state
funds—as in Yugoslavia and East Germany—have played a more
important part than foreign gifts in rebuilding the destroyed or
damaged churches. According to a dispatch of the Hungarian
Church Press in 1951, 546 out of 585 Protestant church buildings
had been repaired or replaced at an expenditure of 58 million
forints (nearly 5 million dollars) of which 43 million were raised
by the churches, 3 million came from churches abroad, and 12
million came from the government. All bodies—Reformed, Lutheran, Methodist, Baptist, and Unitarian—profited by these grants.
The regular budget for aid to the Protestant churches, not including aid to institutions, runs to more than 5 million dollars annually
and takes into consideration the rise in the cost of living.

Lutheran Bishop Lajos Ordass, one of the truly thrilling figures
in the drama of the Christian struggle, still receives a very modest
pension in his enforced retirement. Cardinal Mindzenty at the time

of his arrest and trial, reputedly drew from the state a salary twice as large as that of the prime minister! It is doubtful whether any other state was quite as generous in its fiscal allocations to the churches as the Hungarian Communist regime led by a militant atheist.

It is apparent that these satellite regimes have followed quite a different anti-religious policy from that pursued in the early days of the USSR. It is also apparent that such a policy would not be adopted without Moscow's clear permission; nay, insistence. In the absence of any full, official explanation for it, the true reasons for the policy must be pieced together.

Firstly, the Kremlin has not been converted, except perhaps to the wisdom of using religion rather than opposing it. The war seems to have convinced the Kremlin leaders not only that in distress people cling stubbornly to their faith in God but that religion has, even from the Soviet standpoint, a temporary national and social value. Therefore, let the church live, but let it be harnessed to the Communist chariot.

Secondly, the church must not be permitted to impede the progress of the social revolution, and must therefore pay a stiff price for the support and protection it gets. There will be no frontal attacks against the Christian faith as such, and no godless societies supported by the state on a par with the churches. But the church must sacrifice its extensive properties and private income; also its public power, including educational and welfare establishments; and even—as a precaution—its right to develop its new "freedom" according to its own convictions. In Warsaw, as soon as a wooden cross was erected atop the restored cupola of the great Lutheran Church in the very center of the city, government authorities first sawed off the cross and then persuaded church officials to give the building to the state as a Communist center.

In brief, the church behind the Iron Curtain has lost all the immunities that for centuries it had enjoyed in the name of religion, but its basic financial requirements are still being met.[1]

THE "LIBERATED" CHURCH LOSES ITS INDEPENDENCE

In all the satellite states (except Eastern Germany) the clergy have sooner or later sworn an oath of allegiance to the new regime, not altogether unlike the oaths required by certain Western democracies of their state pastors.[2] Every step of the way, it must be made clear, has been accompanied by terror, arrests, detentions, public trials, deportations, and all the other apparatus of police-state methods. The outstanding Protestant trial was that of Bishop Ordass of Budapest, who was falsely charged with currency exchange irregularities. He was found guilty, imprisoned by the state, and then deposed from office by the "progressive" wing in the Lutheran Church. There is no way of knowing the total number of clergy, especially Roman Catholics, who have sacrificed their liberty or indeed their lives since the end of the war in Eastern Europe. Always the issue was declared to be political and, in fact, it has rarely been purely religious. How could it be otherwise in face of a fanatical system of secular salvation?

However, the cause of Christianity has not been helped by some undeniable signs of political and economic side interests, especially in the outstanding examples of martyrdom. The trial of Cardinal Mindzenty, for example, was occasioned by his opposition to the

---

[1] In no important instance, so far as I know, has any established church volunteered to renounce its state subsidy in return for greater freedom, and it is doubtful whether such a gesture would make any difference in its status.

[2] The following oath is required in Hungary: "I (name), swear that I will be loyal to the Hungarian Peoples' Republic, the people, and the constitution and constitutional laws, that I will protect the security of the state, serve the interests of the people within my competence, and in everything endeavor as effectively as I can to foster the strengthening and development of the Hungarian Peoples' Republic."

nationalization of the church schools despite government assurances that compulsory religious education would be continued.[1] Many spurious issues were dragged in—such as letters written to the American Embassy—but Mindzenty's real opposition to the regime was concentrated in his efforts to protect the church's vast estates from land reform, to retain control of education, and incidentally to keep alive the dream of a Roman Catholic state, preferably a monarchy.

One of the most startling aspects of this episode is that the Prince-Cardinal's conviction in court evoked far less public reaction in Hungary than, for example, the arrest of Martin Niemoeller by Adolf Hitler in 1937. Two and one-half years after the Mindzenty trial and shortly after the arrest and conviction of Archbishop Groesz, the Hungarian Catholic leaders, headed by Archbishop Czapik, went to the Parliament building in Budapest to swear allegiance to the Peoples' Republic.

In Poland and Czechoslovakia, the coordinated resistance of the high church authorities has, to all intents and purposes, been broken. In Poland and Rumania the largest Uniat bodies, which provided the Vatican with its best argument that the Catholic Church is genuinely universal and not merely Latin, have been rudely detached from Rome and attached to Moscow. But this reorientation toward Moscow affected the autocephalous Orthodox even more. For many generations Moscow has been regarded in the Orthodox world as the spiritual successor to Constantinople (after it fell to the Turks) and, therefore, as the third Rome. Most of the autonomous Orthodox churches have always conceded a spiritual primacy to the Moscow Patriarchate even though, for

[1] Compulsory religious instruction in the nationalized schools has, in fact, been discontinued, and the churches—as in East Germany—have been faced with the task of setting up children's Bible classes.

political reasons involving national prestige, they have never acknowledged this primacy in actual practice. Now as a result of the greater East Europe co-prosperity sphere policy (to borrow a Japanese imperialistic term), the national Orthodox churches are apparently on their way to becoming full satellites of the Russian church, whether their leaders like it or not.

Bulgaria provides a good example of what happened to the autonomy of an Orthodox church that prided itself on living in symphony with the state. Separation of church and state became official in December, 1947. Instead of granting freedom to the church, however, the new law proclaimed individual religious liberty but placed the church under a director of cults in the Foreign Ministry.[1] Then followed the financial pressures of 1948 already described and the subsequent resignation of the Exarch. From then on all priests were permitted by the Holy Synod to become active members of the Fatherland Front, which is the country's Communist party, and the Holy Synod took pains to reassure the regime that it had abandoned all thought of trying to expose the children to Christian propaganda. In the same year the Fraternal Union of Priests subscribed to the government foreign policy as being basically Christian.

In 1949 the new church law was passed by the state. Article 3 states that: "The Bulgarian Orthodox Church is the traditional church of the Bulgarian people and inseparable from their history; as such it is in form, substance, and spirit a popular-democratic church." Yet it becomes clear in a dozen subsequent articles that everything from annual budgets to theological curricula must be submitted to the Foreign Office. The quotation placed at the head

[1] Art. 78 of the Constitution states, "Citizens are assured of freedom of conscience, of religion, and of the exercise of religious rites. . . . It is forbidden to misuse the church and religion for political purposes and to set up political organizations on religious bases."

of this chapter is worth contemplating. No schools, hospitals, nor orphanages may be operated by the Peoples' Church.

About the same time, the Director of Cults proposed some basic reforms, but the proposals stirred up such a furor in the church that the Foreign Minister repudiated them as unofficial. Finally the Holy Synod cooperated with the Foreign Office in drawing up a new statute for itself that went into force in 1951 and called into existence a National Church Council to share its authority. To sum up: While considerable freedom remains to the Holy Synod on paper, and the Exarchate has been promoted to a Patriarchate, two new factors will in fact control the "autonomous" church: namely, the Foreign Office and the Moscow patriarch.

The fate of "foreign" churches in Bulgaria, being tiny minority bodies, was much worse. In the first place, the church law of 1949 banned groups with headquarters outside the country, which was strange considering the fact that all religious organizations had been placed under the Foreign Office! In 1950 all Roman Catholic leaders were arrested for being in possession of firearms. Nearly two years earlier the much smaller band of 15 leading Protestant pastors had been taken into custody on charges of espionage, had been put on trial in March, 1949, and triumphantly proved guilty by a Communist court. It was a ludicrous demonstration of the deliberate violation of justice. Communism either fondles the religious minorities as counterweights to the big churches (as in Poland) or attacks them first in order to perfect its technique (as in Hungary).

One of the largest Protestant bodies behind the Iron Curtain, the Lutheran Church of Slovakia (400,000) adopted a new constitution in November, 1951, to replace the old one of 1921. The chief changes are that it now declares itself to be "under the protection and supreme supervision of the state" and that "the

duty of the church toward the state is: to support the rebuilding
effort of the people's democratic state and, by moral and religious
instruction, to help the state to create a moral man in the spirit
of Christ. . . . Therefore, the church receives moral and physical
support from the state according to its laws."

CAN COLLABORATING CHRISTIANS COPE WITH COMMUNISM?

It seems fairly obvious that it is not to the technical legal
status of the state-church relationship itself that one must look to
find the real differences between the church in the East and in
the West but to the spirit behind these constitutions and laws. In
both East and West the statutory provisions may be rather liberal,
and in both instances the governments may be hostile toward the
church. At the Iron Curtain, however, the Christian meets for the
first time a militant ideology that is bent on the construction of a
new social order in which, when completed, the Christian church
will have no place. This, and not the question of subsidies, church
schools, and property rights, is the main issue. And it is at this
point that the church, by and large, reveals its appalling weakness.

Evidence regarding the extent to which the churchmen of Eastern Europe have actually tried to come to grips with this staggering
proposition—Christianity versus communism—is much more scanty
than information about church life itself or about these church-state
relationships. It is easy to divide all churchmen behind the Iron
Curtain into three general classes: the relatively few conscienceless
opportunists, the relatively few stubborn reactionaries, and the
broad middle group of those who—briefly or at length—have
wrestled with their Christian consciences regarding their duty to
God, state, and society. What do these wrestlers in the spirit really
think of communism? Conceding that the clock can never be

successfully turned back, how do they view the future? Can they envisage a place for the Christian church in the ultimate new order far beyond these revolutionary times? What sort of new order must it be?

Satisfactory answers to all of these questions are impossible to obtain, but brief insights into the thinking of some leaders are available.

Among those whose profundity of thought may be questioned even though they occupy elevated positions is Mr. Erno Mihalyfi, the present general inspector of the Hungarian Lutheran Church. He is also deputy minister of popular culture under the present regime and general secretary of the Hungarian National Peace Council. Upon being elected to the highest Lutheran lay office in April, 1952, he waxed eloquent in praise of both church and state, but left no doubts about which of the two deserved the greater trust. "I shall endeavor," he declared, "to resist all dangers which may threaten the church, but these dangers can come only from within the church." Men like Mihalyfi can safely be discounted in trying to determine whether the issues at stake for our Christian faith are being carefully weighed, but there are other men whose views cannot be so lightly set aside. We must pray for them especially, both night and day.

Among the few Protestants who have been most vocal during their sincere effort to reconcile the new situation with their Christian faith are Professor Josef Hromadka of Prague and Bishop Bereczky of Budapest. Of course, if they did not say what their governments like to hear, they would not be vocal, but no one who knows them personally will question their integrity and their innate honesty. What they say deserves a thoughtful hearing.

In 1948 at the Amsterdam Assembly of the World Council of Churches, Dr. Hromadka, who belongs to the Church of the Czech

Brethren, expressed clearly his conviction that the West had failed. He said so again in Berlin in 1951. His two concerns are, first, to go back to the "burning" word of God, and second, to see the modern historical process in its brutal vitality. He denies the accusation that in becoming a member of the Czechoslovak Central Committee he has become political; he asserts that he has at last *ceased* to be political. He recognizes himself as a part of the church that has failed. Otherwise, he believes that communism with its ideals for social change, colonial liberty, and world fellowship would not have burst into power. Consequently, he strives to identify himself with actual *events* and not with outworn *illusions,* and it is this identification, he declares, that liberates a man from politics. Actual events today portend the total dissolution of the old world and its liberal values.

Is Dr. Hromadka right and the majority of European churchmen wrong? One of the ablest theologians in Protestantism, he studied in Austria, Germany, and Scotland; taught at both Union Seminary in New York and Princeton Seminary; and is now Dean of the Jan Hus Theological Faculty in Prague. Undoubtedly he is the chief architect of whatever Protestant policy there is toward communism in Czechoslovakia today. Not one minister of the Church of the Czech Brethren, to which he belongs, appears to have had serious difficulties with the state, and the inner life of the church has not been disrupted. The new regime retains the power to confirm all pastoral appointments and pays salaries directly, instead of giving block grants to the central ecclesiastical administration. Both the Czech Brethren and the Slovak Lutherans demurred at this direct financial contact but were not supported by the other large bodies. The assurance was given that pastors were not to be considered as state employees. Up till now, all goes well. The question arises: Can Dr. Hromadka be right?

Bishop Bereczky, like Joseph Hromadka, is impressed with the fault and failure of the church. The core of his theme is repentance. The world's upheaval is the will of God. Christians must pray for pardon, proclaim the gospel, and work for peace. He used to hope that the satellite churches could become the bridge between East and West, but he is now convinced that the West in its blindness does not understand what is going on in the depths of our days. Writing to a peace congress convened in Great Britain, he said in behalf of the Hungarian Reformed Church, "I heartily welcome your peace congress, expressing my wish that English Christianity in its entirety may find its place in the mighty camp of peace-loving mankind."

Upon returning home from his last trip to Switzerland in 1951, he wrote a cordial greeting to Professor Chao of China, who had resigned as one of the six presidents of the World Council of Churches, saying that he, too—Bereczky—could no longer sit as a member of the World Council's Central Committee, after the World Council persisted in holding to its Toronto resolution that justified the UN police action in Korea.

That may be the frail Bishop's last visit to the West. One by one all the contacts are being broken, either voluntarily or involuntarily. And Hungary was the last of the five satellites with which any regular personal contact had been maintained. As for Czecho-slovakia, a journey to Prague, which a few years ago seemed no further than Zurich, is today as remote as Yakutsk. It is not merely a matter of visas, but has definitely become a matter of common language. The jargon of politics has infected all vocabularies, both East and West, to such a degree that soon only those Christians who read the same international press services and listen to the same radios can be reasonably sure that they know what their exchange of words means. In this sense, the rift between East and West, except in Germany which we shall speak of next, is alarmingly complete.

Across this chasm one bridge still holds! But it is neither Hungary nor the Hungarian churches, as Bishop Bereczky hoped. He himself saw it plainly until he became too involved—as we are constantly in danger of doing—with such things as peace appeals, the recognition of Red China, and the international control of the atomic bomb. Such topical matters undoubtedly deserve Christian attention, but not first place. For in giving them first place we no longer comprehend one another. The only link is Jesus Christ—the fact *that he lived,* that he is daily with us, *and that he will come again* in glory. Slowly but surely, the men who believe this to the exclusion of everything else, whether they are in prison for their faith or on the front pages of the Communist press for their "progressiveness," will have their effect. This is the bridge that, it may be hoped, will reach to the Russian Orthodox.

THE RUSSIAN ROME

The road from the Western church to the Russian Orthodox has been cut for a long, long time. Thirty years of silence under the Soviets seems a minor matter when compared with the East-West separation that has lasted approximately ten hundred years. For the last several decades only the Anglican Church has made a sustained effort to stretch the hand of Christian fellowship across this gulf to the great mass of Russian Christians. In 1944 an important Anglican deputation led by the Archbishop of York made a dramatic trip into embattled Russia, but recently these contacts have been confined almost exclusively to the unofficial and personal visits of the so-called Red Dean of Canterbury.[1]

---

[1] Not to be confused with the Archbishop of Canterbury, head of the Anglican communion.

The free churches, of course, kept up a lively correspondence with their own brethren under the Czar, undertook large relief programs in the early 1920's, sent study groups to the USSR under Intourist tutelage. But only on relatively rare occasions have they been able to revisit Russia since the Cold War began.

As far as the Orthodox are concerned, their isolation is partially self-imposed. It all dates back to the Pope's "excommunication" of the Ecumenical Patriarch of Constantinople in 1054, to which reference has already been made. Since then the Orthodox world does not consider that it was expelled from the true church, but holds that it was the Roman Catholics who fell into schism. Seen from this standpoint, the whole Protestant Reformation becomes a sub-split, and all the pieces of Christendom must eventually return, not to Rome, but to the Orthodox Universal Church. The descriptive term "orthodox" means just what it says: namely, *"right teaching"* or *"pure* doctrine."

The oldest symbol of Orthodox unity is the Ecumenical Patriarchate of Constantinople that, happily, has never developed into a rigid monarchical pattern like the Roman Church, but holds to a federal principle: namely, autonomous churches agreeing together. Together they constitute a sort of family council. This conciliar idea has survived until today as an exceedingly strong unifying force even though no Orthodox ecumenical council has met for more than one thousand years.

Laws based on the first ecumenical councils from the fourth to eighth centuries are still in full effect, and the old liturgy remains untouched and unchanged. Some of the Eastern church's most striking characteristics are that priests are permitted to marry, both the bread and wine are given in Communion, and the devout bow but do not genuflect. There is no cult of the Holy Sacrament or the Virgin Mary, who is venerated but never placed on an equal basis with the Trinity, as in contemporary Roman Catholic teaching.

Russia was converted to Christianity less than a century before the great split with Rome occurred. After the original Christian Patriarchates in Antioch, Syria, and Jerusalem dwindled in importance and disappeared in the Moslem world, and Constantinople was made the capital of the Ottoman Empire, the young Slav nation became the chief champion of the "true faith." The Patriarchate was established at Moscow in the sixteenth century to make good Rome's defection, and for three centuries it loomed large in members, wealth, and influence. An abrupt halt was put to its decadent magnificence in 1917 by the Revolution. The doors of its great cathedrals were closed at that time; its tremendous monasteries were abolished; its clergy was ruthlessly hounded, exiled, and slaughtered.

Communism under Lenin's leadership struck Russia and its established church with the full force of a virulent new plague descending upon a community utterly without immunity. In effect, the Russian church alone bore the full brunt of blows that Karl Marx had actually aimed at the only churches he knew: namely, the Protestant and Catholic churches of Western Europe. Someone has aptly said that Eastern totalitarianism is the logical result of Western secularism.

Persecution erupted at intervals until the eve of World War II, when the enfeebled Russian church received a sudden opportunity to make important contributions to the final victory and thus won the right to reinstate itself in public favor. That this has contributed to the milder treatment since accorded to the satellite churches seems certain, but it has had no apparent effect on the severity with which Soviet wrath has descended on the annexed Baltic area.

CHRISTIANITY UNDOUBTEDLY LIVES IN RUSSIA

Today it is impossible to know whether the Moscow Patriarchate is simply the Kremlin's stooge, as some say, or whether it has really arrived at the beginning of a *modus vivendi* in a Communist society. No doubt it has found its footing somewhere between these two extremes. The Moscow Patriarchate is fully aware that the regime is radically atheistic, and "regrets" it.[1] But the church is loyal to Russia, unashamedly prayed for victory in the war, and unhesitatingly receives back the "erring" churches that are brought within its jurisdiction by the expansion of the Soviet frontiers. Toward the end of 1952, Patriarch Alexius, by decree of the Supreme Soviet, received the Order of the Red Banner of Labor "for outstanding patriotic activity." Yet at no point during the past thirty years does the Moscow Patriarchate appear to have wavered from the strict principles of its ancient canon law, but the test of its continued existence will come in its ability to preach the gospel—not merely hold services—in a violently hostile society.

So far as one can surmise, the Christian churches of the USSR are regaining strength slowly but steadily. In 1941—partly for war propaganda purposes no doubt—a few official figures were published, indicating that 30,000 "religious associations" existed in the USSR and that there were 52,442 "ministers of cults," but only 8,338 licensed places of worship. Orthodox churches numbered 4,225, as against 46,459 in 1917. In 1940 there were 37 monasteries instead of 1,026. Two theological academies plus 10 seminaries had taken the place of the 4 academies and 58 seminaries that were dissolved after 1917.

---

[1] The Soviet State Press in a new dictionary of *foreign* words defines religion as: "A fantastic faith in gods, angels, and spirits, without any scientific basis. Religion is sponsored and supported by reactionary elements. It serves to enslave the worker and extend the power of bourgeois exploiters."

Infrequent visitors in recent years report crowded churches and deep spirituality in both the Orthodox and the Baptist services. The English Friends, who made a peace pilgrimage in 1951, said later that 1,800 persons attended an ordinary weeknight Baptist meeting and that 25,000 people flocked to the St. Sergius festival at the famous Zagorsk Monastery near Moscow, which was attended also by the Rumanian and Bulgarian Patriarchs. A Belgian evangelist described crowds of 2,000 coming twice on Sunday to Baptist services in a former Lutheran church, and observed that some of the worshipers knelt during prayers! According to him, the Baptist community numbers 6,000 in Moscow and has 6 pastors, but there is no Baptist seminary in the whole USSR.

To what extent the Orthodox Church is still spreading is difficult to say, but a reliable report issued by the Church of Scotland in May, 1952,[1] estimated that by 1947 the number of Russian bishops had increased to 67, as compared with 28 in 1940 and 130 in 1917. There were also 3 archbishops and the Patriarch. The number of churches had grown, it was stated, to the astounding number of 22,000. Nevertheless, no bookshop may deal in religious literature, and the publishing facilities of the church are severely restricted.

Thoroughgoing Communists deeply distrust all Christians, but especially the Evangelicals who claim to accept the social and economic principles of communism. Protestants in the West are likewise skeptical of the Christian-Communist combination, although they rejoice at all signs of religious vitality in the second generation of the Soviet dictatorship. The cordial and unaffected message that the Russian Baptists sent in response to a letter from the Baptists of Great Britain and Ireland early in 1952, for example, contains no crass propaganda, although it includes a plea for

---

[1] *Report of the Commission on Communism.* It contains much valuable data on various Iron Curtain countries.

information as to what the British churches are doing for world peace.

Speaking of peace, it is not wise to underestimate the ultimate influence of the propaganda in which the USSR and all of its satellites are currently engaging. Communists have made a deliberate practice of adapting many of mankind's finest concepts to their own subversive purposes, thus robbing them of meaning. This is what is happening to the word "peace." Obviously, peace should engage the attention of all Christians, but it has now become the glib motto of the Christian Communists.

In May, 1952, the Patriarch of Moscow assembled people of a considerable array of faiths—Christians (including Catholics, Orthodox, Baptists, Lutherans, and Seventh Day Adventists), Moslems, Jews, and Buddhists—to launch a peace campaign. They declared, "the source of war does not lurk in the USSR . . . but over there, where social contradictions are explained by a surplus of population, where the most effective means of mass destruction of people are being developed, where war is being prepared." The same statement condemned bacteriological warfare and called on the masses of Moslems and Buddhists in "capitalist, colonial, and dependent countries" to shake off their chains. It ended with a message of gratitude to Stalin.

How can Christians have drifted so far apart? When the Iron Curtain has lifted, can we ever find our way together again?

No visitors appear to have reached the newly-incorporated Soviet republics of the Baltic area to see what is happening to the religious life there, but some horrendous reports of the usual deportations, persecutions, and martyrdoms have leaked out. Although the Orthodox churches re-established relations with Moscow, and new Lutheran bishops and archbishops were somehow placed in office, there is every reason to believe that these churches did not escape so easily as the ones in the satellite states. Fantastic rentals must be paid for the use of church property and exorbitant fees for religious ceremonies such as baptisms, weddings, or confirmations. Eighteen thousand Lutheran hymnals were reportedly burned in one country. The Latvian Baptists presumably continue to carry on, if the report that they officially signed the World Peace Council's Stockholm Appeal is to be trusted.

Whether all reports and rumors about daily living conditions in the Soviet Union are true or false, it is an incontrovertible fact that the Christian church behind the Iron Curtain has been subjected to an experience that—at least for Western churchmen—is simply unimaginable. In the face of such suffering, the rest of Christendom must keep its counsel and agree even with churchmen who merit no special respect when they say, "Do not think that you know better than we what we should do!" Brief outbursts of radical communism from Bavaria to Hungary just after World War I or during the Spanish Civil War bear no real resemblance to the long-term problem that in Eastern Europe confronts not only the church but the Christian faith as such. The world indeed seems to have been sawn in half. But it cannot always stay that way. As the late Nikolai Berdyaev, great Russian philosopher-in-exile, said, "The division of the world into two parts is inadmissible for the Christian conscience." It may even be that the long road to a new Christian order will go through Moscow before it ever reaches Rome.

8

The Key to European Peace

It makes no sense whatever for a man to exert himself in behalf of peace on earth, if the roots of his life are grounded in disdain and contempt for God's will. At this point perhaps there is no great difference between East and West.—Bishop Hanns Lilje.

After each lost war Germany is punished for her past with democracy and rewarded with rearmament as a recompense for future services.—Anonymous.

IT HAS frequently been said that if there is no peace in Germany, there can be no peace in Europe. This is a true statement, but its inner truth does not rest in the obvious fact that Germany is a part of Europe. Germany is much more than a part of Europe. Its truth also does not rest on the popular assumption that Germans possess an extraordinary talent for breaking the peace. Like all nationalities, Germans are to a great extent the product of history and of their total environment. The geographical fact is that Germany and the Germans constitute the center—the physical heart—of Europe.

What is known as Central Europe is inhabited by German-speaking peoples, meaning Germany plus Austria.[1] Situated in the middle of the continent, these two related nations have a common

[1] The only other area where German plays an important role as an official language is the northern half of Switzerland.

frontier with ten non-German states, not including the pint-sized principalities of Luxembourg and Liechtenstein. In fact, if you take a thread long enough to reach from the middle of Germany to Norway, it will touch or cover seventeen major countries as you swing at full radius around the map of Europe. But this same thread, which almost brushes Spain, Bulgaria, and Russia, represents little more than an overnight journey in a sleeping car or a hop of three to four hours by plane.

Germany, of course, represents more than the physical middle of Europe, just as any home is more than the sum of all the floor space occupied by a family. For one thing, it holds about one-third of all the Protestants of Europe. Moreover, it is a solid bloc of 68 million highly-compressed people, not counting the 8 million Austrians. The very fact of their central location has enhanced their role in European life.

Every European nation has made a rich and distinctive contribution to the continent, but Germany-Austria's peculiar destiny seems to be that of middleman *par excellence*. Commercially they control a large percentage of the international land routes and riverways that are natural promoters of industry. Politically they are possessed, rightly or wrongly, of a buffer-complex, because until recently they were divided into a multitude of tiny states, each with its own frontiers that were almost as flexible as Japanese screens. Culturally they have been, except for intervals of exaggerated Germanism, a melting pot of all the arts and sciences known to man.

Whether the Germans have performed their central function well or badly is perhaps a matter of debate, but there can be no debate about the fact that they are still crowded together in the very heart and bowels of Europe. Without health in these inward parts, all hope of a healthy and united Europe is a vain delusion.

Health, by Christian standards, is not merely a matter of economics. National Socialism was a militant ideology, and when its totalitarian regime came to an end with the fall of Adolf Hitler, the nation suffered a total collapse. The consequence was the creation of a dangerous vacuum in Central Europe, which, despite all concessions to self-government, was inadequately "occupied" by the victors. One victor has been intent on replacing Nazism with Sovietism, whereas the other victors have made not quite such strenuous efforts either to restore pre-Nazi freedoms or introduce new freedoms of their own.

Both sides have encountered resistance. To what extent can you successfully pour new political ideologies and a new religious faith into a moral and spiritual chaos as you would pour concrete for houses or distribute relief goods to refugees? Or do you take what you find and give it, if good, a new chance to grow? Perhaps in this respect politics and religion are different. Even if the former can be poured on by propaganda, the latter cannot. Fortunately, there was a lot of Christianity left in Germany and Austria amid the rubble. The Nazis' 96 per cent majorities in public plebiscites were even more misleading than the census figures that still register more than 96 per cent of the population as either Catholic or Protestant.

HOW CHRISTIAN IS GERMANY?

Under Hitler all Germans were expected to believe in God, and thus the Führer's first year of power not only put an abrupt stop to church resignations but brought a mighty return of 230,000 persons who had previously resigned. As it became apparent, however, that Christianity and National Socialism were incompatible, the number of new resignations gradually increased from 29,000 in 1934 to 378,000 in 1939. In those six years 1,300,000 people (including children) withdrew from all churches, yet this represented a drop of only 3 per cent in total membership. Today in Western Germany 96.4 per cent of the population belong to some church, and the same figure probably holds for East Germany.

Recently, new efforts have been begun in Western Germany to launch a leave-the-church movement and revive various substitute cults. In Hamburg the number of youngsters "confirmed" outside the church in a sort of socialistic youth dedication rose from 200 in 1946 to 3,000 in 1951. Similar ceremonies are to be seen in both Oslo and Copenhagen. In the North German province of Lower Saxony (population 6 million) the number of resignations from the church rose from 6,000 in 1948 to 13,400 in 1949, proportionately divided among Lutherans, Roman Catholics, and others.[1]

It is generally conceded that most of these people had long since been lost to the church and had never bothered to leave it until economic circumstances, abetted by a slight increase in church taxes, forced the issue. On the other hand, many thousands who had left the church under Nazi pressure have returned since the war's end, thus reducing the net loss. Contrary to the trend after World War I, the return to the church has consistently outnumbered resignations from 1945 to 1949.

[1] Before World War I, resignations from church never rose above 30,000 per year, and during both wars they dropped very low. The following table of figures, when read in the light of modern German history, provides food for thought:

1918	— 8,724	resigned
1919	— 237,687	"
1920	— 313,995	"
1921	— 265,936	"
1924	— 84,169	"
1931	— 243,514	"
1933	— 57,459	"
1934–1935	—	
1937	— 319,708	"
1939	— 377,721	"
1945	— 9,493	"
1949	— 83,695	"

vs. 324,451 returned to church
returns outnumbered resignations!
(Christian conflict with Nazism)

Probably more indicative of Germany's religious condition is the Gallup-like sampling of public opinion early in 1951, according to which 78 per cent of the population actually believe in God, 62 per cent of these believe in Jesus as the Son of God. Fifty-eight per cent of the young people in the age group between sixteen and twenty-five years responded affirmatively, and 75 per cent of those above 65 years.

Startling as these figures may seem at first glance, the chances are that they would stand rather favorable comparison with the actual status of belief in God in the United States, although the American is more apt to pay lip service to the idea of deity.[1] That, of course, does not answer the question as to *how* the Christian faith of this clear majority is applied to public or even private life.

Of what good are such statistics as an index of Christianity? In the Russian Zone, that is, the German Democratic Republic, they may have more significance. The DDR, as it is commonly designated, used to have 17 million Evangelicals, predominantly Lutheran, in a population that was at that time 21 million, thus making it the most important Protestant territory to fall into the Russian orbit.[2] Is it of any significance that 85 per cent of all Protestant children in the first six years of school are still receiving regular Christian instruction under the auspices of the church? Or that a special corps of 15,000 teachers has been trained to help handle this enormous new task that fell to the church when religious instruction was expelled from public schools? Much of this heroic story was told in Chapter Two. Can the Christian training of children in any Communist country be written off as nothing more than

[1] One poll taken in the United States reported that 96 per cent of all Americans believe in God.

[2] East Germany, Estonia, and Latvia are the only Protestant countries under Communist control. Incidentally, the population of the DDR is dwindling away to the West; the latest total is only 17 million.

form and tradition—yes, even where Communists have agreed to let it remain in the public schools?

Such figures become important. They are far more reassuring, for example, than Premier Otto Grotewohl's statement that 70 per cent of the members of his Socialist Unity Party (Communist front) belong to the Christian churches in the DDR. Nevertheless, it would be a mistake to jump to the opposite conclusion: namely, that the final victory is assured. A recent random sampling of 30 persons by a West Berlin newspaper to find out how much they knew about the Ten Commandments elicited the information that only one old man knew them all, whereas two others knew none of them. The remaining 27 persons could usually name one or two commandments, especially those against killing and stealing, but only 5 could recall the First Commandment! Of the same 30 persons, 7 attended church regularly, 7 never went, and the rest went only to baptisms and funerals.

WILL THE CHURCH PROSPER IN ADVERSITY?

It is true that only 10,000 (out of 6 million) members left the Protestant church of Berlin-Brandenburg in 1950 (a smaller percentage than in Lower Saxony in the British Zone), and that this loss was cut most remarkably by the addition of 5,000 adults, but it is obvious that danger threatens the whole Eastern Zone.

Since the end of 1951, there have been 5,434 pastors actively at work in all of Eastern Germany, a truly impressive figure. But they are trying to minister to 6,100 parishes, which means that 12 per cent of parishes are not adequately served, not counting more than 1,000 that were previously abandoned. Moreover, 3,500 of these pastors are carrying a heavy schedule of religious instruction as well, and there are not enough students of theology in the universities of East Germany to fill up the ranks as the older men wear out. An accurate figure for all theological students in 1951 is about 4,600 to 4,700, but only about 750 to 800 are in the East. If the total number were more evenly divided, the needs of the German churches would be fairly well covered. About 13,000 deaconesses and 633 deacons are fully engaged, but here again it is difficult to find new recruits as the old generation retires from service.

For the time being, the DDR is making substantial grants to the church for the reconstruction or repair of "cultural monuments" destroyed or damaged as a result of the war. One pastor says, perhaps with his tongue in his cheek, "The state seems to look on these churches as symbols of great German architecture which must be rebuilt."

A startling picture of recovery is to be seen in West Berlin, which in 1945 had only two undamaged Evangelical churches and has gone through many a crisis since. More than 80 of the remaining 100 Evangelical churches (not counting 12 others that were bombed to bits, destroyed by subsequent weathering, or blown up later) had either been rededicated or were in process of repair. The church losses for all of Germany during the war amounted to at least 1,200 totally destroyed and 6,000 damaged. Comparable losses have been inflicted on the Christian churches in certain other European states, but these totals are worth noting because of the stupendous sums that would be required to replace houses of worship alone. To cap the climax, the church lost all of its accumulated resources in the currency reform of 1948, which completely wiped out bank accounts and savings in order to cope with inflation.

There is an old belief that the church thrives on tribulation. This is not entirely true, because history reveals that some churches have been eradicated by persecution, but there can be no doubt that adversity is frequently a better ally of the living church than too much prosperity. If so, the German church knows that it has at least one strong friend! Within less than twenty years, adversity has brought three major blows: Nazi persecution, total war followed by total defeat, and finally national partition between the democratic West and the Communist East. Consequently, every one of the king-sized problems confronting the churches elsewhere in Europe is present—highly aggravated and intensified—in Germany. For instance, the German church must try to find a *modus vivendi* in two states instead of one, and at the same time—while dissociating itself from either—try to bring them both together again. On top of the recognized need to make some major Christian contribution to the planning of a new social order, the church must help the nation tackle the gigantic problem of integrating 10 to 12 million refugees into an already groaning economy. Above all, it has a spiritual vacuum to fill—equally as great as that which yawned in Central Europe between the Holy Roman Empire and the Turks at the time of the Reformation. Does the German church see this?

CHRISTIANS WEIGH THEIR PUBLIC DUTY

There has always been a certain tendency in the German church to steer clear of controversial public issues and attend strictly to its own theological affairs, or, since the war, to put its own house quietly in order first. If there was ever a time when it might pay to remain as unobtrusive as possible, the time seems to be now. Many a German has the feeling that if he emerges from the faceless crowd for an instant, his name will go into somebody's black book, who, by a vicious twist of fate, may become his last judge on earth. There is, for instance, a remarkably short-sighted inclination in certain quarters to blame only the victors for everything that has happened. This school of thought thrives on the prolonged detention of war prisoners as slave labor or war criminals, on the multitudinous injustices involved in de-nazification, on the dismantling of valuable industrial plants that in many instances might have employed refugees and are now being rebuilt at great expense, and on other obvious imperfections in allied postwar policy.

A few churchmen of this school publicly refer to all Germans who try to do anything whatever—whether in East or West—as Quislings. This viewpoint is by no means widespread, but it is sufficiently strong to intimidate many Germans into holding onto a neutral position out of fear of the future. A couple of years ago the standard answer to almost everything in Germany was, *"Ohne mich!"* (Count me out!) It was based not only on a sense of frustration, futility, and disgust, but to a large extent on fear. Responsible Christian leaders, however, clearly realize the folly of remaining aloof from the course of national events. On the other hand, the Lutheran Church has warned its ministers that if they enter politics, they cannot expect to retain pastoral posts.

The question is largely one of finding the proper medium of expression on public issues. Protestants, including those in the free churches, continue to be hesitant about engaging in political activities along the organized party lines normally followed by Roman Catholics. Despite a distinct difference in method of attack, the relation between the two great confessions is characterized by mutual respect and cordial cooperation. Nowhere else in Europe has such unity of spirit been better expressed in practical Christian solidarity, vividly exemplified in the sharing of each other's churches in innumerable instances all over the refugee-flooded country. This does not eliminate certain fundamental problems that are reserved for the next chapter, but it has been gratifying to know that competent leaders of both communions have labored together constructively in matters of urgent public interest. These range from a new national school policy to the protection of the refugees (including non-German D.P.'s), and the fullest possible restitution of rights and property to Jewish victims of Nazi terror.

More than anything else, the incredible eruption of vicious anti-semitism under the Hitler regime has made the Christian conscience sensitive to its public responsibility. As to what happened to Europe's Jews from 1933 until Nazi rule was smashed in 1945, simple figures are silently eloquent. Where there were a few millions, there are now a few thousands. In cities where there were thousands, you now count them by tens. Many fled in time, others were successfully concealed, and some were rescued at the end, but the vast majority perished and their property was expropriated. Where was Christian Europe while this was happening? Yes, it did much for a few individuals, but it was powerless to prevent the mass horror. What part this memory plays in the effort to make the church a more effective instrument of Christian public policy is difficult to say, but the scars of shame are tender. The slightest signs of reviving anti-semitism in Germany today bring quick public action. Moreover, the West German Government—despite serious threats of economic boycott by the Arab states—is determined to honor its pledge of indemnity to Israel.

COMPLEX PROBLEMS IN A COMPLICATED SETTING

Within the Protestant church there has been both an increase and a decrease in friendly cooperation. Gradually the walls of discrimination against the free churches have fallen away. Methodists, Baptists,[1] and others have in the past had reason for bitterness at

---

[1] In 1952 the Methodist Church reported a total of 65,000 members in Germany, a 30 per cent increase since the war. Forty-one per cent of the total are in the DDR. Baptists also report a considerable increase of adherents, approximately 40,000 adult baptisms since the war's end.

the hostile treatment they have received from the big provincial churches, although sometimes the excessive zeal of free churchmen has led them to use methods that were bound to provoke a strong reaction. Today there is a regular working fellowship of representatives from the combined provincial churches and the union of free churches. The latter also have been included from the very beginning in the joint postwar all-Protestant relief agency known as the Evangelical Hilfswerk.

But within the Evangelical Church in Germany, which comprises the 28 territorial or provincial bodies containing virtually all of the Protestants, there has been an increase of tension between the Lutherans and the Reformed. These tensions are centered in the activities of a wing of the confessing church, under the leadership of Martin Niemoeller and the continuing influence of the Swiss Reformed theologian, Karl Barth. This group is trying to effect: first, a full organic union of the churches by building on the convictions and fellowship that resulted from the Nazi struggle; and second, a reformation of congregational life by a systematic cultivation and enlargement of the living "nucleus" in all the large "deadwood" parishes.

In contrast to this position, the United Lutheran churches wish to conserve a united national front while postponing actual merger until doctrinal agreement regarding the Word and the Sacraments has been reached. To them the Evangelical Church in Germany is not really a church but a federation. The orthodox Lutheran approach, in general, is more conservative in all things, whereas the views of the present leaders in the confessing church—far from being confined to church matters—find constant public expression in virtually every current topic of major interest to the average German: for example, remilitarization, German unity, etc. Neither Niemoeller nor Barth can be described as pro-Communist, but there is no doubt that their radical political utterances have given comfort to the Kremlin.

There is general agreement among all Protestants that the church must contribute actively to the creation of a new social order in Germany, but there is broad disagreement in Western Germany as to how far the church itself should go and what the new order should be. A return to the *status quo ante* Hitler would satisfy many. Others have vague ideas of Utopian improvements. Much more has been done in trying to define the Christian concept of the state than in trying to define the Christian concept of society. Nineteenth century notions of institutional aid to the needy and afflicted continue to dominate Christian social thinking.[1] This pattern will probably be broken soon by the gradual impact of new, vital study centers like the Evangelical academies or the Evangelical School of Social Studies at Friedewald, especially if more pastors continue—following the English example—to explore personally the strange new world of industry and labor.

Meanwhile, at least three crucial new problems are receiving careful thought not only in government offices at Bonn but in Christian circles everywhere: the vast social problem inherent in the reabsorption of millions of homeless people (*heimatlose*) into normal communities; the perplexing problem of redistributing wealth (*lastenausgleich,* literally "equalization of burdens") so as to equalize the very inequitable situations caused by the war; and

[1] In this field the Germans have done excellent work. The Inner Mission reports that in West Germany alone it employs 82,000 professional workers, including 35,000 deaconesses, 4,000 deacons, 2,000 pastors, doctors, and lawyers, and 5,500 welfare workers; there are also 25,000 other employees! In its 276 hospitals, 50 asylums, 360 rest homes, and 680 institutes are a total of more than 100,000 beds. There are 850 additional institutions for the aged, workers, homeless, seamen, and others. Catholic Caritas has an equally good system of institutions. In *all* Germany it has over 4,000 establishments with over 300,000 beds and 80,000 persons employed in full-time service, not counting such things as kindergartens, first-aid stations, and sewing schools.

lastly, a serious endeavor to give labor a representative voice (*mitbestimmungsrecht*) in the management of industry. This last does not mean, as in "Socialist" East Berlin, the privilege of either "volunteering" to clear away rubble after work in the evenings or contributing 3 per cent of wages as a release from extra duty!

Every one of these problems is loaded with social dynamite, involving the possible danger of a bolshevik destruction of old values in an otherwise laudable attempt to create social justice. Can the disinherited be given a fair share in the future without bankrupting the German economy completely? Can millions of refugees be received openly without pauperizing everybody? Can labor become a controlling factor in big industry without destroying private enterprise? On all of these issues Christian opinion is articulate, and so far the reaction is completely affirmative.

BISHOP DIBELIUS: FEARLESS CHAMPION OF THE CHRISTIAN CAUSE

No doubt the most important contribution that the German church can make to the plans for a new social structure at a time when the country is being split asunder is a steadfast defense of the Christian view of the dignity of man in a day when one part of the country is dominated by the technical measuring-stick of each man's economic usefulness. Social schemes that deny the inherent value of the individual, whether they come from the East or the West (and sometimes they come from the West) are basically wrong. Bishop Dibelius of Berlin constantly reiterates this main theme in his public efforts as spokesman of the Evangelical Church Federation to preserve spiritual unity in spite of physical division.

Bishop Dibelius is a church statesman of unusual caliber. He is a scholar whose learning encompasses but goes far beyond theology.

He is an administrator with a strict sense of discipline but whose vision soars over bureaucratic detail. Under the Nazis he was repeatedly arrested, then deposed from office and forbidden to speak. The years have not diminished the courage that he brings to his exposed post in Berlin, subject to attack from all sides but universally respected for his keen perceptions and his rock-like integrity. Some attention has already been given to his views on the state in Chapter Four, but perhaps a brief account of some of the events during the past three years in Eastern Germany will indicate that these Christian convictions are not intended to be stored away in dusty libraries for future generations.

In a Pentecostal letter, dated June 1, 1949, the Bishop spoke to the city and all the congregations in his diocese, saying that for four years the church leaders—remembering Hitler's occupation of Europe—had abstained from public criticism of the occupying forces. But now that a German government was in the making, a new responsibility became apparent. Then he went on to expose the Gestapo methods of the Peoples' Police, the legal injustice of the Peoples' Courts, the mockery of the ballot, and the restrictions on religious freedom. Communist pressure increased, pastors were recruited for the so-called National Front and even for espionage, whereupon the Bishop issued a solemn warning, cautioning them to keep themselves clear of such political entanglements as would endanger the church.

Only a handful of pastors became "progressive," but by October, 1950, both the Catholic and Protestant radio services were terminated voluntarily because the progressive clerics were permitted to broadcast in the place of scheduled preachers. Meanwhile, less than a year after the first letter, the responsible heads of the Berlin-Brandenburg Diocese signed a special message dealing with the deeper conflicts of conscience caused by state policy. Parents, pupils, and teachers, under a barrage of anti-Christian indoctrination in the public schools, were calling for moral support from the church. The letter unequivocally reaffirmed the faith on which Christian fellowship is founded and concluded with this blunt declaration, "This truth is not compatible with the materialistic view of life. We protest, therefore. . . . No governing power has the right to force upon anyone a philosophy that runs counter to his faith and his conscience."

Within a matter of weeks, despite strong public protests, the great steeple of St. George's Church rising high over the Alexanderplatz in East Berlin was deliberately destroyed, and about the same time an editorial appeared in a Communist daily upbraiding the "reactionary" churchmen who "approved the Nazi terror and blessed the arms for Hitler's predatory war." "These church leaders," the editorial continued, "protest against the fact that the universities of the DDR are teaching dialectical materialism as the scientific ideology of the working clasess. They have the benefit of the freedom of theological studies, . . . but they are not prepared to let the working classes have the same freedom, . . . and are trying to persecute the working classes." The editorial also castigated the churchmen for their reactionary attitude toward the persecuted progressive pastors and the "democratic" youth organization.

A few months later, Premier Grotewohl publicly attacked the Protestant church for allegedly giving its approval to the rearmament of Western Germany. "Military propaganda is a crime," he declared. "A militant church, therefore, is impossible in a democratic state."

Young people were forbidden to visit training schools in West Berlin, relief supplies coming from Western Germany were cut off, and an attempt was made to force Bishop Dibelius to move the provincial church headquarters (not the city offices) from West Berlin to the town of Brandenburg, under the threat of stopping further state remittances within a month. This latter measure was taken by the Premier of Brandenburg Province, who declared that it was contrary to the constitutional rights of DDR pastors to be disciplined by church officials who were not even citizens of the same state! Within a week the Premier received a clear-cut reply from Bishop Dibelius in a long letter stating that the only pastor in question had not been disciplined for his political views, that the church stood on its constitutional rights to run its own affairs as it saw best, and that if the reunion of Germany occurred soon, as was so ardently desired by all parties concerned, the question of moving the offices would become superfluous.

Any attempt to make it appear that the Bishop was hiding in West Berlin was ridiculous in view of the fact that he openly preached regularly at the Marienkirche in the East Sector, but the Premier put pressure on all pastors in the province to vote for a change of headquarters at the synod meeting in February, 1951, and threatened to set up a puppet regime if they refused. The synod stood solidly (226 to 1) against any transfer, suggesting only that official meetings might be held alternately in East and West Berlin. Moreover, they charged the state with unwarranted interference in the life of the church.

Instead of taking further steps against the church, the Communist authorities preferred to ignore this rebuttal and instead lauded the synod for a strong resolution pleading for German unity and supporting the Bishop in his endeavors to mediate between the West and East governments, which he had sincerely tried to do. Financial subsidies were not discontinued, the progressive clergymen were quietly forgotten by everyone, and the same summer the great Kirchentag assembled in Berlin with the full cooperation of the Communist DDR regime, which, while it apparently has no intention of persecuting the church, remains firmly committed to the principle of cutting the ground from under it, exactly as Hitler tried to do.

PEACE IS INDIVISIBLE

If there is one single reason, above all others, that accounts for the relatively solicitous behavior of the Communist regime in East Germany toward the Christian church, it is certainly the hope of achieving a reunion of the country on Communist terms, which means under Communist control. If hopes of reunion continue to fade, the church is likely to suffer accordingly.[1] But assuming that this supposition is reasonably correct, a brilliant floodlight is thrown out over the whole Soviet religious strategy in the satellite states, revealing a policy designed to postpone the final showdown with Christianity until the conquest of Europe is complete, which was also Nazi policy.

There is no good reason to believe that communism will ever tolerate Christianity longer than absolutely necessary, and it behooves the Christian church to make the most of the opportunity it presently enjoys not merely to foil communism but to change it. For, the same floodlight thrown forward seems to promise that if the USSR should ever succeed in subduing the rest of the continent, Marxism-Leninism will very likely have some ugly surprises left even for the Patriarch of Moscow, to say nothing of Protes-

---

[1] The change in the status of West Germany between the summer of 1951 and the summer of 1952 was reflected in the DDR's attitude toward Christian youth rallies. Suddenly on the eve of two big outdoor youth conferences in different parts of East Germany, long after official permissions were secured, the Christian youth organization was declared "illegal" and the meetings called off. All arrangements to transport and accommodate the hundreds of youngsters were cancelled. Even private hospitality was restricted and spied on, but it appears that everybody concerned defied the police and the rallies occurred as planned.

tantism's progressive pastors, who in reconciling their Christian faith with communism are yet a long way from reconciling communism to the Christian religion. In more ways than one, therefore, the churches of divided Berlin stand not only between the East and the West, but between the past and the future.

To evaluate the importance of Berlin for the future of the Christian faith in Europe, a brief excursion into recent history is essential. The Russian aim to dominate all of Europe in the postwar period was not generally acknowledged in many reluctant quarters until Czechoslovakia capitulated to Communist pressure in February, 1948, just ten years after Hitler had made abundantly clear his own intentions of European mastery by swallowing Prague. The second conquest of Prague proved to be both the high water mark of the Communist advance into Western Europe and the turning point of the Cold War. In quick succession came the futile attempt to win the Italian elections in April (see p. 106) and the vain effort to capture Berlin by isolation. This latter maneuver really began with the first road traffic interdictions in March, 1948, and led to a long and costly year of supplying the besieged city from the air.

These two major defeats seem to have caused Soviet strategy to reverse itself, for the next important step was to launch from Stockholm a vast peace campaign while transferring Kremlin attention to Asia. The blockade of Berlin had been lifted less than a year when war broke out in Korea, but Communist pressure on the old German capital has never abated. As Red President Wilhelm Pieck of the DDR said in welcoming the Kirchentag in 1951, "Berlin today is for all Germans the symbol of the struggle for unity and peace in our homeland. For this reason the Church Congress has also chosen the German capital for its meeting, so that over and above the unity of the Christian faith the unity of Germany may also be recognized."

Christians admittedly constitute a natural audience for peace appeals. As reported in the preceding chapter, the Patriarch of Moscow is aware of this. It is nothing to be ashamed of. The very notion that the Communists should be the first to make big political propaganda out of the world's yearning for peace was enough to make many Christians most uncomfortable about their anti-Communist position. It was like reading the flat pronouncement in the constitutions of all the Peoples' Democracies that hate is henceforward forbidden, thus apparently achieving by law a goal that the church through love had never reached. Only when the cauldrons of Soviet satellite invective were poured on Tito's head did the meaninglessness of this particular legal prohibition become fully apparent.

Nevertheless, in East Germany the formula is persistently applied: peace and unity! The sound of these words is seductively sweet to the German ear. The church naturally wants peace and unity also, with all its heart. As a willing or unwilling partner, the Protestant church would obviously make an admirable stalking horse for the *Pax Russiana,* owing to its possession of the only effective bridgeheads on either side of Germany's Iron Curtain. As a consequence of its strategic position and the popular appeal of the peace crusade, the church can neither speak up nor remain silent without being accused of political interference. German church leaders are, for the most part, fully aware of both the danger and the responsibility inherent in this situation, and some of them, like Bishop Dibelius, are also aware of a golden Christian opportunity.

The biggest danger is that German unity—quite aside from its intrinsic urgency—may be made the object of national and international power politics. If this should happen, the church could no longer express its convictions without being branded as a partisan of some political viewpoint. This day is fast approaching. The measure of Bishop Dibelius' statesmanship is to be seen in the front-page editorial that he published in the *Berliner Sonntagsblatt* on May 25, 1952. He wrote:

We shall not permit it to be turned into a political issue! I mean, the reunion of Germany. The longer it goes on like this, the more party politics enters the picture. Soon it will be so bad that if you talk about reunion in the West, people will look on you as pro-Russian. And if you talk about it in the East, they will say you are Adenauer's tool. We of the church are not interested in politics of that sort.

The Berlin Bishop went on to inveigh against the unnatural separation of families and the emplacement of armed troops along the border drawn through the center of the country, but concluded with the ringing declaration, "There must be no war for the reunion of Germany!"

In this tragic situation the Christian church has so far played a noble and helpful role. Cannot more be done? Is the world-wide church doing all it can?

Despite the fact that the church as a possible pawn of power politics is in a most awkward and delicate dilemma, it seems positively providential that the Iron Curtain, which cut the continent in half when the conquest of Europe failed, also cut Germany—the middleman!—in two. For one thing, if the division had not occurred, no gap would have been left in Europe's Chinese Wall, which probably would have been built even higher and more impenetrable, and the churches behind it would have been still worse off. Do not imagine that things could not be worse than they are! In fact, the division of Germany into two countries threatened to become permanent in 1952. This would probably sunder the hitherto united church.

Meanwhile, the unremitting effort to unify Germany—which Germans fortunately will never abandon—may even point the way to the reunion of Europe, *if* it does not land us all in another World War.[1] What I am trying to say is simply this: the key to real peace is European unity and the key to European unity is German unity. These problems of unification cannot be solved by occasional UN pronouncements or pious phrases, but only by indefatigable hard work, plus a passion for a cause. It could conceivably happen that, without a divided Germany, the world would gradually take a divided Europe for granted until the big crash came between the USSR and the USA. But the division of Germany holds out the thin edge of hope that human ingenuity—backed by prayer and driven by a German refusal to accept the split—may yet find a workable solution, and therewith a formula for peace.

MARTIN NIEMOELLER AND THE QUESTION OF GERMAN UNITY

Let us not be deceived! The debate about the reunion of Germany's two halves has only just begun. If the division should continue as long as the partition of Poland lasted, that is for 150 years, the debate will go on. Agitation, unrest, and bloodshed will never cease. In other words, there will be no peace in Europe while the present separation continues. On the other hand, all ill-considered efforts to end the separation may only make matters worse. Pastor Martin Niemoeller has been quoted as saying that he would prefer union under the Soviets to an intolerable disunion. This and other similarly startling utterances turned the spot-

---

[1] It is self evident that the division of Germany at the Elbe—that is, into two zones—carries the seeds of conflict, but it is no less obvious that an even greater potential cause of war, if these two parts of Germany were free and united, has its roots in the Oder-Neisse Border, for this marks the *de facto* annexation of whole German provinces by Poland. Germany is really divided into three parts: West, East, and Polish-Russian!

light of hostile attention on Niemoeller, once heralded as the champion of Christian freedom under Hitler. Contemporary newspapers are so puzzled that they hardly know whether to call him a Nazi-at-heart or a would-be Communist. He is neither.

First of all it must be said that Martin Niemoeller is a prophet in the Old Testament tradition and prophets do not fit into political pigeonholes. Jeremiah and Jonah also had a logic all their own; yet God was in them and he would not let them go. Only posterity can fully judge the role that the former Dahlem pastor, now president of the Church of Hesse-Nassau and the head of the German Church Federation's foreign office, will have played in our generation. More than anyone else Pastor Niemoeller has hammered away at the guilt of the church; more than anyone else he resisted the first signs of German militarization, warned of the inevitable consequences of the East-West split, and pleaded for both Christian and political reunion. Was not that what everybody wanted? But more than any other man he has caused dissension both at home and abroad. Why? Well, partly because of the timing and the manner of his interventions, which seemed calculated only to provide grist for the Communist mill.

Prophets sometimes betray a weakness for saying the wrong thing at the right time or the right thing at the wrong time. Niemoeller was placarded all over the Russian Zone as a progressive pastor and held up as an example of the way clergymen should behave. Finally, eleven pastors at tremendous risk wrote an open letter to their brethren in the West stating that the DDR around them was full of concentration camps containing tens of thousands of Germans. Had Niemoeller forgotten what that meant? All children were being systematically trained away from Christianity and pressed into Soviet service. The East Zone longed for liberation, they said, but everybody knows that another war is not the answer. They declared their conviction that voluntary military defense training in the West was infinitely preferable to the kind of forced labor that would result if the Soviet Army overran the West! Hundreds of thousands of East Germans had already been drafted into the people's police and were being instructed in tank units and heavy artillery! The strength of the West is our only hope, they concluded. Germany needs not only to be reunited but to be defended.

Pastor Niemoeller is far from being insensitive to these ugly realities, but nothing prevents him from obeying the dictates of his conscience. Early in 1952 he accepted an invitation to visit Moscow to meet the leaders of the Orthodox and Baptist Churches. According to his own report of the brief visit, he found intense spiritual vitality there, and he also found himself at odds with the local Peace Committee. He discussed questions of major interest to Germans—for example, the release of prisoners of war still held in the USSR—and also problems of vital importance to the Christian church at large, such as closer relations between Russian Orthodoxy and the ecumenical movement. Yet his trip was violently criticized both inside and outside Germany. Bishop Dibelius, as president of the Evangelical Church Council, found himself in the difficult position of both defending Niemoeller's motives and dissociating himself from his political views.

A little later in 1952, Dr. Niemoller was invited to return for the Church Peace Conference over which Patriarch Alexis was to preside and to which reference has already been made. In declining the invitation, the German pastor expressed his hope that the conference would truly serve the cause of peace. The most interesting passages of his long letter ran as follows:

Rarely in all my life have I found a decision so painful, because on the one hand I do not wish to let slip any opportunity of serving . . .

the cause of peace among men, and on the other I have to be equally concerned not to destroy and annihilate by overzealous action the degree of mutual understanding between men in East and West which God has been allowing to grow up. . . . This is the difficulty which now confronts me. It will not have gone unnoticed by you that, while my visit to Moscow met with much approval and little criticism in the American public, it aroused much hostility in Western Germany and all over Western Germany, and for the time being it is my principal concern to combat this hostility. . . . It is this that I regard as being, for the moment, my most urgent task.

There can be no doubt that both the invitation and its reply were motivated by a genuine desire to serve the cause of world peace.

Later in the same year Bishop Dibelius, head of the German church, received an invitation from the Patriarch to come to Moscow. With Bishops Lilje of Hannover and Hahn of Saxony, he planned the trip in November, 1952. Asked for an explanation of his proposed visit, the Bishop of Berlin said significantly, "The church of Russia has come very close to us. It is time that all the churches should establish contact with one another." Asked whether he was not fearful that his trip would be misconstrued politically, he cheerfully replied, "I am sure of it!" One thing is certain: Bishop Dibelius won't lightly be accused of communism. Unlike Niemoeller, he is not interested in the so-called Peace Congresses. Owing presumably to a speech that the Bishop delivered in London shortly before his scheduled departure for Moscow, the Patriarch suddenly became indisposed, and the trip had to be postponed.

This much must certainly be said for Dr. Niemoeller's controversial behavior: he dared to challenge practically every crucial postwar issue that stood in danger of being handled on the hush-hush level of power politics, and he forced public discussion. This applies especially to clandestine remilitarization and to the passive acceptance of a divided Germany. In the old-fashioned sense of the word, Martin Niemoeller is neither a man of the cloth nor a man of the world, but a man of God, which does not mean that he has always been right, nor that he is necessarily a diplomat, a statesman, or an administrator. But in his passionate desire for the reunion of Germany as an indispensable prerequisite for peace, there has been constant danger that rash behavior would, if carried too far, bring not peace but the sword.

No other national church, as is abundantly clear from the European survey we have made, is so deeply involved in the whirling vortex of the world's postwar problems. Here in Germany, especially in East Germany, peace is not an abstract concept but something so real that it daily affects the life of each individual. Lack of peace intrudes into every home with the same abrupt reality as illness, hunger, unemployment, or sudden death. It is far more than an academic matter of agreeing to a well formulated resolution or affixing a signature to somebody's petition to be filed and perhaps forgotten. It is no exaggeration to say that the problem of peace in the Russian Zone comes to the Christian in the following forms: "Shall I prepare my child to live as a Christian, even though he goes to a concentration camp; or shall I let the state train him for a 'normal' life in a Communist society?" "Shall I spy on my friends so that my husband will be sent home sooner from Siberia?" "Am I unwittingly promoting war or peace by expressing my ardent longing to see my country reunited again?"

BRETHREN STANDING IN NEED OF PRAYER AND GUIDANCE

What sort of guidance can the church give on questions of this sort? In June, 1951, there was to be a big plebiscite in the DDR on the issue of rearmament, and it was taken for granted that the citizens would vote 100 per cent against rearmament and in favor of peace. The East German regime's Department for Church Affairs sent an open letter to all clergymen expressing the expectation that Christian pastors would take a "positive" attitude toward the plebiscite, and warning that anyone attempting to dissuade voters from going to the polls would be suspect as favoring an American war policy. Christians who were acutely conscious of the one-sided propaganda purposes to which the Stockholm peace appeal had been put were in a serious dilemma. How should they vote? Once more the Evangelical Church of Berlin-Brandenburg sent out a message reviewing the various statements against war that the church had made. Then it said: "The Christian who takes part in the plebiscite and answers with 'Yes,' addresses himself thereby to the competent authority in his *own* state and warns against any production of weapons of mass murder and against training in the use of them."

In other words, the ballot was to be deprived of its propaganda value outside the DDR without endangering the voters' status on the question of real peace. A few months earlier the Lutheran Church of Saxony had spoken its mind on the subject of the Stockholm peace manifesto: "We see in the fanaticism of the World Peace Movement a faith in the redemption of the world without God and without Christ, through scientific socialism. Its methods of revolutionary class struggle and war we regard as irreconcilable with the divine commandment to love. Its hope to create by its own virtue a state of affairs where there will be no more crises, no more wars, no more misery, is in our eyes a political sentimentality playing on people's religious feelings." The province of Saxony, it may be added, reportedly contains, by Communist standards, only 13 "reliable" clergymen among 1,458 Protestant pastors and Catholic priests!

The church all over Germany ardently wants peace, but it was exceedingly hard, after Europe was divided between hostile powers, to take a position against rearmament. Bishop Dibelius has publicly said—and Pastor Niemoeller, too, but in utterances often subject to misinterpretation—that the church is opposed to it *both* in the East *and* in the West. He has also said that West Germany cannot be expected, without protection, idly to watch the rise of "police forces" in Eastern Germany. To most Germans it seemed obvious that the ultimate participation of the West German Federal Republic in the Western European defense forces was inevitable, and now the great debate on this aspect of the subject is as good as closed. From now on the debate will revolve around the question as to whether it should ever have been permitted to happen!

The German people are not entirely happy, but they seem to derive some satisfaction from the distinction between remilitarization and rearmament. The former idea conjures up the nightmare of the old war-machine; the latter bespeaks a partnership in the North Atlantic Treaty Organization. Whether it is a distinction without a difference will depend, as far as inner German developments are concerned, on the church's ability to blaze a new trail out of the vicious historical circle in which the nation is caught. Germany is not out of that circle yet!

There is perhaps one concluding word to be said on this whole subject. It is contained in the quotation from Bishop Lilje that heads this chapter. What is the point in laboring for peace, he asks, if man's life is firmly rooted in disobedience to God's will? War with God is incompatible with peace on earth. Civil order at its best can do no more than provide a guard against chaos and disorder, as Martin Luther pointed out in his Doctrine of the Two Kingdoms. It cannot bring salvation. But today *two* civil orders are engaged in deadly combat for the whole body of Germany. Therefore it has become urgently necessary that Christian thought be absolutely clear regarding the relation of the two kingdoms to each other. All temptation to consider the civil order as an authority—or divinity!—in itself, and therefore beyond God's reach must now be recognized for what it is, state worship. If that is the sort of kingdom the Germans want, they have the DDR. But, from the Christian point of view, as Luther clearly taught, the civil order, too, is subject to God and must obey his will. It does not mean that the state is subject to the church or to any earthly official of the church, but to the word of God.

As to the present state of the church itself, considerable attention is being paid in Eastern Germany to the inadequacy of old ecclesiastical forms. Something is obviously wrong with a church that, as an institution for the propagation of eternal truth, finds such a thin echo in the hearts of Christendom's bewildered grandchildren. Even before the end of the war, the impact of Hitlerism had set a few bold Christians to wondering whether the time had not come to build a different sort of Christian fellowship. Dietrich Bonhoeffer, able young theologian whose life was cut short in a concentration camp on the eve of the Nazi collapse, became convinced that religion as we know it today is merely the "garment of Christianity," but not its body. Too much of our modern church has been revealed as a hollow shell. What has happened to its contents?

Across the Oder-Neisse line a very few pastors and some consecrated laymen are trying to minister to the scattered remnants of once-flourishing German communities. To the average American the roster of German cities east of Berlin may sound almost as strange as Astrakhan, Tiflis, and Samarkand, but to Germans it is inconceivable that Stettin, which had 240,000 people (all German), now is called Szczecin and has 74,000 people (mostly Poles), or that Breslau, which had 800,000 (practically all Germans), now has only 168,000 (almost all Poles) and is called Wroclaw. Roman Catholics in this region have requisitioned most of the Protestant churches whether vacated or not, and, as we saw, are now committed to support Poland's claim to these German provinces, but the real masters of the situation for the moment are the political commissars. Seen from Berlin the area east of the Oder-Neisse line is, religiously speaking, a swept and garnished house. Its rightful inhabitants have been driven into exile. Hardly a shell of the church is left.

Is that to be the destiny of Western Europe also? Or can what is left of Eastern Germany—where even the circulation of periodicals from the West is prohibited—point the way to the triumph of Christianity in the one area of Europe where, humanly speaking, communism today has the upper hand but the power of the church to compete with it has not been completely broken?

9

The Abrahamic Adventure

It was by faith that Abraham obeyed his call to go forth to a place which he would receive as an inheritance; he went forth, although he did not know where he was to go.—Hebrews 11:8.

WHEN Walter Lange got home from Russia long after the war was over, he found a job in a West German automobile factory employing 20,000 people. The work was fine, but Lange was a Christian and the whole atmosphere of the shop troubled him. His efforts to draw his new friends into serious conversation earned him rebuffs, smiles, and the nickname of "departmental Christian"; but his skill and intelligence brought him promotion to one of the special machines, which was a badge of success. One day during the lunch hour, the Christian was put next to a rabid Communist, who was an expert at flaying the church. In the ensuing argument, Lange stood his ground, and shortly thereafter a Catholic came to him suggesting that the Christians get together.

Within six months, nearly 1,500 men and women of all departments had organized themselves into a nucleus to discuss company policy and workers' problems from a Christian viewpoint. Arrangements were made for 180 pastors and church officials to visit the plant and see the world in which the workers lived eight hours each day. One of the by-products of this tour was that 20 of the pastors volunteered to spend four weeks working as replacements for 80 men who wished to participate in Christian retreats and conferences! Then came the annual plant election. The Workers' Council was traditionally composed of 26 trusty Marxists, most of whom were Communists. Without difficulty the new Christian nucleus garnered 50 per cent of the votes and took 12 seats in the council.

It would not have been too difficult to fill these chapters with stories like this, but the effect might have been misleading. Although the number of Walter Langes in Europe is relatively large, it is by no means large enough to warrant the assumption that an endless repetition of his splendid example would gradually solve the problems of the world. There are also churchmen like Bishop Gulin of Finland, who has made an effort to visit every plant in his Tampere diocese, which is known as a little Pittsburgh. While work stops for a half-hour the Bishop talks to the employees and then shakes hands with them all.

The Finns, already half surrounded by the USSR and at one time within a hair's breadth of going completely Communist, are today vitally aware of the basic importance of the Christian faith. Over in Norway, the Gallup Institute discovered that religious programs on the state radio are next in popularity to the news broadcasts and light music. Bishop Smemo of Oslo says that it is easier to interest the youth of Norway in the activities of Christian societies than in political parties. Down in Rome, a city abounding in churches, groups of 20 to 30 people have begun to meet in private homes to hear Catholic laymen, or perhaps a priest, discuss some article of faith with a view to making the influence of Christianity felt as an effective factor in the daily life of those who have drifted away from the church.

LIVING TABERNACLES

These few examples are extremely encouraging as signs of Christendom's residual vigor—the warm embers under the ashes of a fire that is by no means dead—but what hope do they hold out for the Sunday church? Does the cumulative evidence of hand-picked examples of religious vitality prove that the church itself is fully alive, or simply that the Christian faith is still a driving force in the daily lives of numbers of individuals?

In trying to answer this question, which is not too well stated, attention must first be drawn to the fact that the examples given above are not indicative of life *inside* the church with which most of us are familiar. They describe religious life *outside* the church, at least in the old institutional sense of the word. It is probably true that if several thousand more Walter Langes would stand their ground, the church would undoubtedly experience a limited revival, could even take honest credit for some of the results; but its own perplexing dilemma would not be solved, because it *is* a dilemma and not simply a problem in arithmetic. That is to say, the church is not faced with a problem that can be solved solely by the addition of more members or by the multiplication of their religious activities.

The whole of the church of Christ is more than the sum of all its parts and members, and there is no doubt that the spiritual condition of Europe today constitutes an appeal to the *whole* church, even in its present divided state, to stand its ground in relation to the *whole* of life and try to do in the world what one man accomplished in an automobile factory. It is a matter of creative witness. This the church is not yet fully doing. But the church as such cannot be blamed for failure, since the church does not exist apart from its members. Obviously, its work can be done only through individuals and by individuals who are strongly reinforced by *a divine sense of community* and who are moved by the Holy Spirit.

Therefore, while it is true that individuals are *in* the church and, consequently, parts of it, it is also true that the essence of the whole church is *in* each Christian individual. He is much more than a member of it. The most significant phenomenon of modern Europe, religiously speaking, is that so many Christians have come to realize that the church is within them wherever they go, even into camp or exile. This is a new concept of the communion of saints. It is no longer an external object fitted with a steeple and attached to a plot of ground that is usually filled with graves. Those who found this new, invisible fellowship in camp or exile are no longer satisfied with the Sunday church; they need the church daily in the factory, office, and the home.

No iota of spiritual pride attaches itself to the solemn realization that the member *is* the church. On the contrary, it is suffused with a profound sense of awe and humility. How could it be otherwise when the physical destruction of the vast institution that used to be known as the church left the still-living member standing before a broken building with the quivering remnants of his faith in his hands, asking himself, "Is the church destroyed?" The answer was No. The members who saw their clergy taken captive, whether by body into concentration camp or by spirit into an alien ideology, found themselves facing a similar question: "Does this dissolve my church?" The answer again was No.

It was the search for these answers that led both clergy and laity to the conviction that the Christian fellowship was not housed solely beneath Gothic arches and fostered only by men in special vestments. Thus, in a time of incredible humiliation, subjected as he has been to all the inhumanities of his fellowmen, the consciousness of a new dignity began to awaken in the Christian man. The church is *in* him. He does not become part of this fellowship either by belonging to the church and paying a tax or by withdrawing from the official church to found a sect. Yet he still belongs to society. You cannot escape from it. It is becoming increasingly clear in Europe that *church and the whole community belong together*. Whereas the old concept of the church had lost the warmth of community fellowship, the new concept of community fellowship requires the purpose and discipline of organized religion, especially in the face of organized irreligion.

There is no doubt that many millions of Western Europeans once thought of themselves as having moved on ahead of the church. In a sense, they had done so, but not without having had to accept some ideological substitute for it, even though they retained the idea that they were still Christians. But now, thanks to a minority of its members, the church itself is beginning to get under way, and neither the stages nor the end of its journey are apparent. The fact that humanity itself is perceptibly moving again is probably the most significant phenomenon of our times, and the church must move with it. How far the Sunday church will venture beyond its present ecclesiastical confines has not yet become apparent, but it cannot stay where it is. A static church is of little use in the world today except as a wayside shrine. Wayside shrines undoubtedly have a beauty and an importance of their own, but their chief spiritual value resides not so much in the piety that put them there as in the piety of the traveler who trudges past today and tomorrow. The church that the migrant carries with him is far more important than the church that he leaves behind; and it is of the utmost importance that an Abrahamic sense of religious adventure—of going out, not knowing whither it is going—should possess the European church again.

THE NEED FOR A NEW COLLECTIVE WITNESS

This demand for a venturesome faith places a new responsibility upon Christian men and women to *be* the church in the midst of the world and to push out the narrow boundaries that distinguish the Christian fellowship from the larger human fellowship and that divide Christians from one another. But it is at this point that every Christian discovers the weakness of the church in himself: namely, an inability to communicate Christianity easily to his own fellowmen. That is why the Walter Langes are relatively rare. Old evangelistic techniques, as was pointed out in Chapter Two, are virtually useless, because the modern non-Christian as a rule detects in himself no special need of the sort of fellowship that the average church has to offer. He won't come to the church, and the church as an institution cannot reach him, except perhaps as a humanitarian agency. Only the sincere Christian who can prove his witness by his work is acceptable to the world.

Whether or not the whole Sunday church can then follow the sincere pioneer depends on the extent to which it is ready to take seriously the questions that Dietrich Bonhoeffer mulled over in the last weeks before his martyr's death in Nazi Germany: "Are there such things as Christians with no religion?" "In what way are we an *ecclesia*[1] without believing ourselves to be especially favored but as belonging wholly to the world?"

These are exceedingly difficult questions to answer, but some churchmen in Europe have begun to see that new forms of collective witness must be developed to correspond with the new forms of individual witness. Just as the priest-workman, for example, must empty himself of his physical church and its ingrown fellowship, the witnessing church must empty itself, wherever necessary,

[1] Greek for church, meaning those who are "called out."

of its institutional substance in order to become again a spiritual fellowship.

Strangely enough, the new individual feeling of being the church is today making for unity rather than disunity. After all, it—that is, the feeling of being the church—is not really so new and radical as it may seem to those who in this generation are experiencing for the first time in their own lives the rough and merciful hand of the living God. But whereas nineteenth century individualism in its intense search for personal salvation was frequently divisive and sectarian, twentieth century individualism is impregnated with a strong sense of common destiny and, in the tangled confusion of postwar Europe, tends to produce order rather than disorder.

The factor that drives men together is to be found in society's forward movement toward an unknown destination. This is most clearly seen among the refugees on the road, in their camps and in their journeys to new countries. Entire populations are on the march both physically and spiritually. If they have not been bodily uprooted from one part of the world and transplanted in another, the probability is that they have at least been pushed from one ideology to another by whatever party comes to power. Deprived of former familiar landmarks, many of these spiritual DP's, motivated not by some individualistic notion of salvation but by a desperate desire for guidance and fresh strength, seize hold of their Bibles. And it is this that confirms in them a new feeling of solidarity and common purpose, even while, at the same time, union (or merger) remains as difficult as ever.

Indeed, the antitheses between the various sections of the church are as sharp as ever, if not sharper. In certain quarters it was inevitable that the antagonism should even increase as the depth of doctrinal differences became apparent in the light of the Bible itself. Of course, not all of the differences are traceable to the

Bible. Most of them are rooted in human causes. Consequently, Bishop Berggrav declared that our aim should be to set Christendom right in ourselves and our churches before using it to set the world right.

Physician, heal thyself! There can be no doubt that the chief drawback to a common Christian attack on the problems that surround the church is division within the church. Christendom, if it can be said to exist at all, is certainly not united, and—despite the imminent threat of conquest by communism—the prospect of unity is no greater in Europe than elsewhere in the world. Thus it is not entirely true to say that we are living in an ecumenical era, although it can be said that ecumenicity is increasing. In certain respects, it is a "limited ecumenicity" insofar as it also expresses itself in a national or denominational sense; that is, in union movements of a regional or confessional nature. In the postwar period all of these movements, by and large, are contributing to the larger ecumenicity, not detracting from it. On the whole, it may be said that *if* Christendom ever takes form again, it will not be as an amorphous mass of citizens enrolled in churches or groups of churches, but rather as a fellowship of individuals conscious of having chosen personally between Christianity and some form of non-Christianity.

CHRISTIAN LIBERTY AND CHRISTIAN RESPONSIBILITY MUST MARRY!

It is true that communism has been an effective factor in bringing Christians to recognize the basic faith they hold in common, but it has also been a divisive factor because it has provoked divergent views regarding the form that Christian opposition should take. Many Christians have accepted the idea that entrenched communism can be met only with force, either economic or military. This attitude, which appears to be reflected in Vatican policy, is based on the assumption that non-Communist world powers—of which the Vatican State considers itself to be one—must combine in a crusade to contain or defeat the Kremlin. In other words, Christianity should make political alliances.

From a purely political standpoint, it is obvious that the nations of the world must work out their policies and procedures (with or without Christian influence) in the light of the existence of the USSR and its Communist partners. It is also obvious that Christianity cannot absolve itself of responsibility for what happens when this is done. However, it is not so obvious that the church itself should deliberately seek its allies on this level.

Other Christians find a different idea more acceptable: namely, that by an assiduous application of Christian faith and action—both at home and abroad—to the basic issues themselves, solutions may be found that neither communism nor any other ideology can possibly provide. It is disturbing that the Christian church has been more successful in helping to wage wars than in achieving peace. After all, the defeat of communism or fascism is less important than the elimination of conditions that they set out to cure.

While it is true that unarmed Christian faith did not defeat the Nazi Army in war, it is also true that neither military, political, nor economic power can ensure peace. Postwar events abundantly illustrate this thesis. Although this second point of view cannot be claimed as an exclusively Protestant approach, let alone policy, there is no doubt that diverging political views present one of the greatest practical obstacles to Christian unity.

The crux of the matter is the relation of church to state, to which no fully satisfactory answer has yet been found. Certainly not the Roman Catholic answer, as reflected for example in the encyclical of Pope Leo XIII, which assigns final and absolute authority to the Roman Church and rejects the principle of democratic equality as well as the equal treatment of religious faiths. On the other hand, there can be no doubt that complete separation, unattended by adequate Christian safeguards anchored in a responsible church, makes for the swift de-Christianization of society and directly contributes to the growth of political totalitarianism.[1] Perhaps the perfect answer—somewhere between separation and establishment—will never be found.

As we have seen in Chapter Five, there are at least two distinct trends evident in Europe, or at least in European Protestantism—one moving away from state churchism toward separation and the other moving away from separation toward greater Christian participation in the molding of national life. The two are not mutually contradictory. The former is in line with the natural demands of religious liberty, whereas the latter acknowledges the requirements of Christian responsibility. In order to convert these movements into a truly creative relation between the church and the formal framework of society, which is the state, the whole church must be prepared, if necessary, to revise its ideas regarding its own function in the world. This can be done if all the churches bring their contributions, particularly their deepest convictions, to the common task. At the risk of oversimplification, it is worth saying specifically at this point that the Roman Catholic Church needs to review its ideas regarding human liberty and the Protestant church its ideas regarding Christian responsibility.

FRIENDSHIP THROUGH THE CHURCHES!

Despite certain basic differences, the relations between Protestants and Catholics in most European countries remain friendly. There is, however, little or no hope of closer *rapprochement* across the

---

[1] The urgent necessity for developing an adequate system of religious education by the churches in East Germany is a case in point. See Chapter Eight.

top of the great divide that separates the Vatican on the one hand and the Moscow Patriarchate on the other hand from the rest of the Christian world. The existence of unusual groups in Catholicism—such as the Monastery of Union in Belgium that for twenty-five years has fostered better ecumenical relations—must be accepted as welcome evidence of the fact that in certain Catholic circles the desire for contact exists. Yet British Catholics just across the channel cannot obtain official permission to discuss questions of religious liberty with Anglicans or other Protestants. Roman Catholicism itself is by no means of one mind. The report that certain Roman cardinals are directly or indirectly responsible for violent attacks on Protestant minorities in Spain should not be read without remembering that in France a Roman Catholic abbé instituted a Week of Prayer for Christian Unity during which prayers of penitence were offered for "acts of unlawful violence by us Catholics against our Protestant brethren."

Protestants should also know that one Catholic bishop in southwestern France, after being released from wartime internment, publicly paid a debt of gratitude to his Protestant friends for opening the Bible to him; they should know that a group of priests in Paris read mass on the Feast of St. Bartholomew for the Huguenots slaughtered in 1572 and for their Protestant descendants today; that there is, in addition to the growing tendency on the part of Catholic historians to examine more objectively the redoubtable career of Martin Luther, a proposal by one German Catholic scholar to revise—with Lutheran scholars—Luther's famous translation of the Bible in order to provide Germany with one standard version. This would have the double virtue of preventing the repetition of a public incident in Vienna, where the burning of Protestant Bibles was recommended recently in a religious paper because of alleged inaccuracies and omissions in translation!

In order that none of these incidents should be exaggerated out of proportion to actual importance, two cautioning words must accompany them. First, that all evidences of Catholic good will—together with their Protestant equivalents—should receive intensive cultivation in the unflagging hope that essential differences may yet become the seed-bed of unity. And, secondly, it would be disastrous if an era of hostility were followed by a united front that was nothing more than an anti-Communist façade.

Berlin is, least of all, a place where Christians can afford to wrangle with each other. Relations between the Protestant majority and the Roman minority have, in fact, been extraordinarily good since the struggle with the Nazis. Yet Bishop Dibelius' weekly, *Die Kirche,* did not hesitate in the midst of its trouble with the Communist regime to ask why no Catholic paper either dared to deny the facts of Protestant persecution in Spain or to protest against it. The Berlin Catholic paper replied with the suggestion that Christians should stand together today, not attack each other. Whereupon the Protestant paper charged the *Petrusblatt* with sidestepping the real question and added that "where the Protestant church is needed, Catholics speak of a united front; but where the Roman Church has the power, Protestants become heretics to be stamped out by every possible means."

In other words, the predicament in which Christians stand today is all of a piece and no valid line of distinction can be drawn between abuses that are practiced in favor of one church as compared with the same abuses practiced in favor of another church or a political system. This applies equally in Spain, Sweden, or Soviet Russia. Incidentally, Bishop Dibelius later called upon the Protestant homes in Berlin to open their doors to the Catholic pilgrims coming to the mammoth Katholikentag, and he himself had the Roman Catholic Archbishop of Munich as his house guest.

MOSCOW: THE ACID TEST OF CHRISTIAN AMITY

Assuming for purposes of argument that the Catholic and Protestant churches of the West are aligned in a united front, can they regard the Orthodox Church of Russia and its satellites as a Christian ally behind the Iron Curtain? No serious effort has been made to brand the Orthodox Church as non-Christian, but if by "ally" is meant an ally against Russian communism, the answer would appear to be No, whereas if an alliance against atheism is implied, the answer would seem to be Yes. Are we satisfied with this answer, or were we looking for a political commitment?

Of course, no one really expects the Russian church to launch protests, let alone foment rebellion against the Soviet dictatorship. There is no sign that it wishes to do so, nor any indication that the church is even restive under the restraints that, despite its separation from the state, obviously rest upon it. We are not sufficiently well acquainted with the Christian mentality in Russia to know what this really means, but there is no doubt that our own religious and political feelings are intermingled.

Probably the only reason why we are not tempted to condemn the Russian church as a "traitor" to the Christian cause is that it has always stood too remote from our Western experience to be considered as a vital member of the Christian family. But the instinctive inclination to do so emerges clearly in our easy tendency to regroup all Protestant churchmen in the satellite states into either deserters or friends of the resistance.

The point at issue here is not whether it is wrong for a Christian to let his political and religious convictions influence each other. On the contrary, they should do so! The point is: what is the basis of *Christian* unity and a *Christian* peace? Is it the Four Freedoms, or submission to Rome, or some form of socialism, or faith in Jesus Christ? Although it leaves many problems unsolved, the question when put this way immediately answers itself and underscores the fact that one of the chief reasons why Christians of the world cannot unite is because their religious attitudes have become inseparably linked with familiar social and political systems. This cannot be entirely avoided, of course, but due allowance must accordingly be made.

In this connection, two facts with specific regard to the position of the Russian church are worth keeping in mind: namely, that complete separation from the state gives ultimate promise of greater independence than the church had under the Czars, and secondly, that within severe limits it is already proceeding to reorganize its own internal life. Meanwhile the Orthodox Church in exile has become a little better acquainted with the churches of the West and they with it. Disregarding the political aspects of the situation for a moment, it seems that the possibilities of an eventual coming together look brighter today than ever before, except perhaps for a period of premature brotherhood during the war.

EUROPEAN CHURCHES IN THE ECUMENICAL CURRENT

The problems militating against Christian unity cannot by any means be localized in Rome and Moscow. Protestantism is full of them. Whereas the extent of divergent opinions within the Roman Catholic Church may effectively be screened by an appearance of unanimity on all points, the rifts in Protestantism are public knowledge, revealing themselves in the existence of separate churches, to say nothing of problems exposed daily in the public press. Efforts to establish one major Protestant church in postwar Germany failed to produce a satisfactory basis on which Lutheran and Reformed bodies could really unite. Similar efforts to inaugurate a reunion movement in England have now been limited, at the tactful suggestion of the Archbishop of Canterbury, to the establishment of closer relations between the churches.

The most important result of the modern ecumenical movement, which has been influencing Protestant—and also Orthodox—thought and action in Europe for more than forty years, is that the various churches are gradually getting better acquainted with one another and, by sweeping aside the prejudices and misconceptions that frequently were the main reason for alienation, have got down to the real differences that divide them. The careful settlement of these differences is important because they affect the substance of faith itself. To gloss them over with gestures of good will would—as in the case of the Roman Catholic Church—seriously blunt the edge of Christian conviction when keenness is required.

It is not the purpose of this book to go into the details of the profound theological problems that underlie confessional differences. Suffice it to say that such questions as that of infant baptism —which was hotly debated in the Reformed churches of Europe in consequence of the desire to rebuild truly Christian congregations—go to the core of the Christian faith. So does the question of intercommunion, which, for example, has been the main barrier between the Church of England and full altar fellowship with other non-Roman bodies. This is a Lutheran problem, too.

Mention has been made of the Orthodox conviction that it considers itself to be the one true church and of the difficulty experienced by the Greek church in deciding to participate in the work of the World Council of Churches on an equal basis with the other churches that it does not recognize as true. The free churches of Europe seriously doubt the effect of close association with the state-tied bodies that, in their view, are not free to preach the word of God as they should.

To suggest that these various bodies should simply forget their differences and get together is as naive and unrealistic as to propose all families living in single houses should build themselves one vast barn and dwell in it together. On the other hand, the proposal to work together in unity and with a sense of common endeavor is both sensible and sane.

Indeed, in this respect many churches have already got together in a most remarkable way with the founding of the World Council of Churches at Amsterdam in 1948. The Council has become the meeting place of more than 150 Protestant and Orthodox churches and is prepared to act for them in whatever tasks are delegated to it. These common tasks range from the study of theological problems to the resettlement of refugees in all parts of the world. The existence of the World Council has abundantly proved that churches can live and work in considerable unison despite the historical, national, linguistic, political, and economic differences that tend to isolate their members from contact with one another. It is no exaggeration to say that the greatest deterrents to Christian fellowship are not matters of conviction, but human inertia or resistance to change and the preoccupation of most church leaders with the ongoing problems of their particular offices.

In becoming a meeting place of the churches, the World Council and the other ecumenical agencies, whether confessional or interdenominational, have become more than points of contact and cooperation. They are international in the fullest sense of the word, rising over the narrower frontiers that tend to bind and blind their constituent members. To this extent they represent a universal point of view, which in the case of the World Council embraces the turbaned priest of the ancient Mar Thoma Church of India as well as the gaitered Anglican bishop or the sack-suited editor of an American church weekly.

Even more exacting at present is the necessity of keeping contact as long as it is spiritually possible to do so with the member churches in the Soviet sphere of influence. Often an international organization not only possesses more prestige but can preserve a much greater degree of neutrality in the face of national pressures. The ultimate purpose of supra-frontier relationships is not to glorify any particular form of ecclesiastical organization or to protect vested interests, but rather to broaden the base of Christian fellowship and facilitate the search for common answers to common problems.

More can hardly be said at this point about the World Council for fear of giving the impression that it is primarily a European organization. The fact that its headquarters are located in Geneva actually serves to obscure the necessity for a much greater degree of constructive cooperation among the continental churches. Unfortunately there is no European council of churches to concentrate on the problems that we have been discussing and that unquestionably call for an agency half-way between those separate organizations limited to purely national interests and the one that deals with world affairs. The fate of such a body would probably be that of the Council of Europe, which lives very much in the shadow of the United Nations. Nevertheless, it would be a serious mistake to lend any encouragement to the idea that the World Council of Churches or any other global church agency in any sense relieves either its member churches or the church members of their local or regional responsibilities, least of all in Europe.

THE FIVE MAJOR ISSUES

The urgent task of the church both in whole and in part is to resume its proper place in the world without waiting for universal answers. In none of the areas of Europe that have been briefly surveyed in this book can it be said that the relevance of the church to its world is fully demonstrated. The churches are not even relevant to one another! To be quite specific at this point, and avoid the subtle danger of indulging in pious generalities, it might be well to cast a summary glance at the major issues that have emerged from the foregoing chapters. In general outline, on a chapter by chapter basis, they can be summarized in the following manner.

Europe is its own largest mission field. This constitutes both a problem and an opportunity. The first signs of a new evangelistic approach are taking recognizable shape amid the debris of a shattered continent. This is encouraging because, as we saw in Chapter Three, what happens in Europe is of utmost importance to Christendom, owing to the extraordinary role played by so small a continent in world history. Suppose Europe ceased to be Christian, even in the formal sense of the word?

The church today is seriously hampered by the fact that it has lost touch with the world around it. In attempting to readjust itself, the church of Christ faces at least five crucial tests, which were sketchily described in five successive chapters: namely, (1) its ability to impart a decisive Christian influence to the reordering of society; (2) its ability to establish a genuinely creative relation to the state; (3) its ability to make an impact on international affairs without engaging in ecclesiastical power politics; (4) its ability to confront the menace of atheistic communism at close quarters; (5) and its ability to point the way to world peace.

These are not five completely separate and isolated issues, but five facets of the same major problem, which meets the church not only in Europe but everywhere in the world: namely, the effective proclamation of the gospel of Christ. Proclamation, of course, does not necessarily mean preaching, nor does the word effective apply only to the filling of churches on Sunday! To reduce the problem still further, there are at least two general points of contact with European culture that need considerable clarification: (1) the place where the church meets the state; and (2) the place where the church meets society. Today these are two aspects of the same thing.

As far as the relation between church and state are concerned, we have seen the problem under two lights: namely, in northern and southern Europe. As far as the relation between church and society is concerned, we have looked at it in the "democratic" West and the "democratic" East. Despite the various degrees of influence prevailing in different countries, *at no point can it be said that Christian conviction—divorced from political pretension—is giving decisive direction to the trend of events in Europe.* This is the most serious thing that can be said about Europe today. But not about Europe only!

Looking back over these few postwar years, nothing seems to have turned out as we had anticipated. This applies also to our Christian hopes for the postwar world. None of man's spiritual problems has been permanently solved, although in some instances they have been superseded by other problems of even greater perplexity and urgency. Instead of moving at a headlong clip over some well paved surface toward permanent peace (as some had hoped) or toward complete chaos (as some had feared), we seem to be condemned by Providence—perhaps for not being able to decide which of the two goals we seek—to continue stumbling across the broken country of confusion.

Do the fabled highways leading to peace and chaos actually exist? The fact that all our forefathers pursued the same uneven course between the two should lead us to ask ourselves whether chaos and peace are not the conditions in which we travel rather than the destinations toward which we tend. At any rate, the church, like a tabernacle, is being borne along in humanity's procession as we travel slowly forward under the hand of God. There may be comfort in this: Although swift victory does not come easily to the church of Christ and its members, neither does swift defeat.

This would appear to be an unnecessarily grim note on which to conclude a report from Christian Europe. The prospect of defeat, even if it does not come swiftly, is by no means pleasant. Moreover, an instinctive optimism forbids us to think that God, who sacrificed his Son for the salvation of men, gladly permits any part of his church to disappear. Christian history, right in Europe, reveals several junctures at which total destruction seemed imminent but never materialized. On the other hand, the history of the church in so-called Bible lands and in North Africa, or in the old Japan, to say nothing of the new China, plainly indicates that our towers of Babel *can* be utterly thrown down; floods of wrath *can* cover the earth; even our Jerusalems are *not* indispensable to God. Europe certainly holds no divine guarantee that it will survive this century in its present form.

If these words are unduly somber, they are written in the ardent hope that the destiny of a continent that Christianity made great will not be equally somber. A brighter outlook depends upon the answer given to the issues facing the European Christians and their churches today. It depends upon fanning into large fires of repentance and renewal the small sparks that undoubtedly glow like the campfires amid a slumbering army all over the dark face of the old world. Nor is this a purely European affair. For Europe today is merely one segment of the front that stands in need of the assurance that the whole of Christendom is ready not only to come to its defense, but to help it in launching irresistible crusades of love for the conquest of the world in the name of Jesus Christ. Therefore, the state of the Christian church in Europe is the business of Christians all over the world.

Reading List

NOTE: The subject matter of each book and article listed below is relevant to the chapters of *Report from Christian Europe* indicated in parentheses.

BOOKS

Assignment to Austerity, by Herbert L. Matthews and E. C. Matthews. Indianapolis, Bobbs Merrill Co., 1950. (Ch. 4)

Christian Churches of the East, The, by Donald Atwater. Milwaukee, Bruce Publishing Co., 1948. (Ch. 7)

Christian Year Book, 1950, The. London, Student Christian Movement Press, 1950. (General)

Christianity Today, edited by H. S. Leiper. New York, Morehouse-Gorham Co., 1947. (General)

Church and State in England, by Cyril Garbett. New York, The Macmillan Co., 1950. (Chs. 4 and 5)

Fight of the Norwegian Church against Nazism, The, by Bjarne Höye and T. M. Ager. New York, The Macmillan Co., 1943. (Ch. 5)

Fruits of Fascism, The, by Herbert L. Matthews. New York, Harcourt, Brace and Co., 1943. (Ch. 6)

God's Underground, by Father George (pseud.). New York, Appleton-Century-Crofts, Inc., 1949. (Ch. 7)

Man and State, by Eivind Berggrav. Philadelphia, Muhlenberg Press, 1951. (Ch. 5)

People, Church and State in Modern Russia, by Paul Anderson. New York, The Macmillan Co., 1944. (Ch. 7)

Religion in Soviet Russia, by N. S. Timasheff. London, Sheed and Ward, Inc., 1942. (Ch. 7)

Religious Liberty, by M. Searle Bates. New York, Harper and Brothers, 1945.

State of Europe, The, by Howard K. Smith. New York, Alfred A. Knopf Co., 1951. (General)

Struggle of the Dutch Church, The, edited by W. A. Visser 't Hooft, New York, American Commission for the World Council of Churches, 1945. (Chs. 4 and 5)

Tito and Goliath, by H. F. Armstrong. New York, The Macmillan Co., 1951. (Ch. 7)

Truth about Religion in Russia, The, issued by the Orthodox Eastern Church, Russian. London, Hutchinson and Co., Ltd., 1942. (Ch. 7)

William Temple's Teaching, by A. E. Baker. Philadelphia, Westminster Press, 1951. (Ch. 4)

MAGAZINE ARTICLES

"Acid Test: The Industrial Worker, The," by Eric Fenn, in *The Ecumenical Review,* Autumn, 1949. (Ch. 2)

"Church and State" issue of *The Frontier,* March, 1952. (Ch. 5)

"Church, Russia, and the West, The," by Martin Wight, in *The Ecumenical Review,* Autumn, 1948. (Ch. 7)

"Comment on Democracy" issue of *The Student World,* Third Quarter, 1947. (Ch. 3)

"Effect of Revivals on the Church of Finland," by Toivo Harjunpaa, in *The Lutheran World Review,* October, 1948. (Ch. 2)

"Evangelization of Man in Modern Mass Society, The," by J. C. Hoekendijk, in *The Ecumenical Review,* Winter, 1950. (Ch. 2)

"Evangelism in France," *Bulletin of the World Council of Churches,* December, 1951. (Ch. 2)

"God in an Irreligious World," by Dietrich Bonhoeffer, in *The Ecumenical Review,* January, 1952. (Ch. 9)

"Luther's Doctrine of the Two Kingdoms," by A. Nygren, in *The Ecumenical Review,* Spring, 1949. (Ch. 5)

"On the Relation of Church and State," by Yrjo J. E. Alanen, in *The Lutheran World Review,* July, 1949. (Ch. 5)

"Position of the Church in the Eastern Zone, The," by Otto Dibelius, in *The Ecumenical Review,* Winter, 1950. (Ch. 7)

"Unity of Christendom in the Strife between East and West, The," by Nicholas Berdyaev, in *The Ecumenical Review,* Autumn, 1948. (Ch. 9)

"Regeneration of Europe, The," by W. A. Visser 't Hooft, in *The Student World,* Third Quarter, 1949. (Ch. 3)

Index

THE AUTHOR

DR. STEWART WINFIELD HERMAN was born in a parsonage in Harrisburg, Pennsylvania. He received degrees from Gettysburg College and Gettysburg Theological Seminary, was ordained in the United Lutheran Church of America, and did postgraduate study in the universities of Strasbourg, France, and Göttingen and Berlin, Germany. He was honored with the degree of Litt.D. from Gettysburg College in 1945.

Dr. Herman has spent most of the past seventeen years in Europe. He was pastor of the interdenominational American Church in Berlin, Germany, from 1936 to 1941. From the outbreak of World War II until Pearl Harbor, he also served as a member of the American Embassy staff there. Later, he joined the Office of Strategic Services of the United States Government, and spent the last two years of the war in London.

He helped to initiate the postwar program of Christian relief and reconstruction sponsored by the World Council of Churches. In 1948, he became director of the newly-created Lutheran World Federation Service to Refugees, with headquarters in Geneva. He returned to the United States in 1952 to become executive secretary of the Division of Latin American Cooperation of the National Lutheran Council and the Latin American Committee of the Lutheran World Federation.

THE ARTIST

JOHANNES TROYER, who designed the cover, was born in the South Tyrol. He studied in Munich and Vienna and lived in Austria until Hitler invaded that country. Then he moved to the little principality of Liechtenstein where, for ten years, he designed postage stamps. He later lived for a time in Switzerland. Mr. Troyer came to the United States in 1949 and has since worked for many publishers as illustrator, designer of book jackets, and calligrapher.

THE FORMAT

The text of this book is set in Linotype Granjon, a type face designed by the English printer, George W. Jones, and drawing its basic design from the classic Garamond sources.

The book was composed, printed, and bound by American Book–Stratford Press, of New York. The jacket, paper cover, and endpapers were printed by Turck and Reinfeld, Inc., of New York. The text stock is Warren's No. 66 Antique Book.

Typographic design by Margery W. Smith

Binding by Louise E. Jefferson